LETTERS FROM A

FATHER

TO HIS

BELOVED SON

Dear Pastor Sung woong Lee

Feb. 2009

Daniel K. Lee

LETTERS FROM A
FATHER
TO HIS
BELOVED SON

DANIEL
KYUYONG LEE

Pleasant Word
A Division of WINEPRESS PUBLISHING

Pleasant Word (a division of WinePress Publishing, PO Box 428, Enumclaw, WA 98022) functions only as book publisher. As such, the ultimate design, content, editorial accuracy, and views expressed or implied in this work are those of the author.

Unless otherwise noted, all Scriptures are taken from the *Holy Bible, New International Version®, NIV®*. Copyright © 1973, 1978, 1984 by the International Bible Society. Used by permission of Zondervan. All rights reserved.

Scripture references marked KJV are taken from the *King James Version* of the Bible.

Scripture references marked NASB are taken from the *New American Standard Bible,* © 1960, 1963, 1968, 1971, 1972, 1973, 1975, 1977 by The Lockman Foundation. Used by permission.

ISBN 13: 978-1-4141-1225-1
ISBN 10: 1-4141-1225-4
Library of Congress Catalog Card Number: 2008903345

CONTENTS

Section Three: True Neighbor

Section Four: Praise the Lord

FOREWORD

LIFE, IT HAS been said, is a journey. If we can make this journey with the wisdom and guidance of good spiritual habits established in youth, we will live a life with few regrets. Unfortunately, the world swirls with chaos and fosters confusion, encouraging young people to be materialistic and pursue unrestrained self-interest.

How important it is, then, to have fathers who are willing and capable of passing on good spiritual habits to their sons. I am thankful to God that our church has such a father in Daniel Lee. Although Daniel travels to Manhattan every morning, works hard all day, and comes home late at night exhausted and with tired eyes, he still manages to be a good father to his beloved son.

Like all good fathers, Daniel planted the seeds of good habits in his son's heart, knowing that what took root in childhood and adolescence would eventually flower in adulthood. Now he wants to share with other young men the same habits of heart that he imparted to his own son: love of God and neighbor, honesty, courage, humility, gratitude, and prayer.

It is my sincere hope and prayer that this book will guide young adults in their life's journey, helping them to live a meaningful life even in—no, especially in—the midst of the most difficult circumstances. The most precious gift a father can give to his son is a faithful heart. I recommend this book to all families and pray that God will lead this family and all the families of the world to inherit the good habits of a faithful heart so that they can live a blessed life.

—Pastor **Koo-Yong Na**
Korean Community Church of NJ-UMC

PREFACE

ALL PARENTS WANT their children to live the best possible life. We hope they can live humbly and wisely at all times and with clear goals laid out before them.

> Which of you, if his son asks for bread, will give him a stone? Or if he asks for a fish, will give him a snake? If you, then, though you are evil, know how to give good gifts to your children, how much more will your Father in heaven give good gifts to those who ask him!
>
> —Matthew 7:9-11 NIV

The preceding scripture describes well the desire we have as parents to provide for our children.

I am the father of one son, Kevin, a young man who recently finished his college studies and is ready to take his first steps into the larger world. This book is my gift to him, an attempt to impart a bit of spiritual wisdom to him and all youth like him who find themselves faced with the sudden challenge of making their way in this world.

I have seen many parents work hard their entire lives to pass on their financial fortunes to their children. But it is far better to give your children a spiritual inheritance rather than material wealth—a spiritual inheritance of knowing God, the God who watches over our lives and who has counted the very hairs of our heads. That is why I have written this book.

Looking back on my own life, I see the many mistakes I have made. These mistakes initially made me hesitate to write such a religious-minded book. However, upon reflection, I realized that in those mistakes lay lessons that could benefit my son, and so I decided to leave this book for him and other young men like him.

In my youth, although I attended church, my attitude was still self-centered and world-centered. I wandered here and there seeking worldly experience, hoping to find the purpose of life—one truth upon which I could base my life. But through much suffering, I came to understand that worldly pleasures are always followed by great loneliness and emptiness. It is only after truly accepting God that my life was renewed, that I have been filled with joy, hope, and peace. Not surprisingly, I became less self-centered and world-centered, and more God-centered.

To this day I am still witnessing God's miracles, seeing firsthand the amazing things He does in my own life and in the lives of those I know. For this reason, today's young people should carry within them a hope and a vision for the future. No matter how difficult the circumstances may be, we need to be assured in our faith that God is with us, knowing what is best for us more than we know ourselves. When we understand and accept this, we can begin to live the life that God wants for us.

I have written this book with a prayerful heart to those young people standing on the threshold of adulthood to encourage them to be guided in their journey by the everlasting light of faith.

ACKNOWLEDGMENTS

I THANK MS. Gloria Yoo for her devotion to seeing this book through. I especially thank Sandy Yi and John Schneider for their many hours spent translating and editing, respectively. Also, I greatly appreciate the work of Heeyoung Kim, whose beautiful illustrations greatly enhance the quality of this book.

I cannot thank enough my advisor, Mr. Leonard Adler, who has been practicing law for more than fifty years, and Professor Chongku Chon, a longtime friend, for their personal support and encouragement.

I would like to share my joy at the completion of this book with Pastor Koo-Yong Na and his wife. I owe Pastor Na a debt of thanks for writing the introduction, but more importantly for enriching my spiritual life. Thank you also to my fellow members of the church.

I also thank my dear wife, Jungsoon, for her excellent advice as well as her help in organizing and typing the manuscript, and my beloved son, Kevin, who has grown into a fine young man who makes his father proud.

Most of all, I offer my utmost gratitude and glory to my Lord for the example of love He provides and for His ever-present grace in my life.

—Daniel Kyuyong Lee,
2008

Section One
Always Be Prepared

Chapter 1

WALK WITH GOD

MY BELOVED SON,

As the earth rotates around the sun, the sunflower turns its head to follow the sun. Just as the fish cannot leave water and live, men cannot leave God and live. To set the mind on the flesh is death, but to set the mind on the Spirit is life and peace.

Life is like a sailboat in the middle of the ocean. In the course of its voyage, it may sometimes find itself making great speed with a tailwind, but more often than not it may sail directly into a headwind, being buffeted by fierce wind and waves. We need to be assured in faith that God is with us every moment of our journey. We must put our trust in Him until we finish our journey. Trusting in Him gives us courage and confidence to overcome hardships and obstacles, however difficult they may be.

Negative thoughts, discouragement, and timidity deprive us of the ability to tackle our problems, which leads to frustration of our will. If we consider ourselves weak and small, it will become a self-fulfilling prophecy. But if we have confidence and pride in being children of God, we will be able to deal with any and all adversity. People with a positive attitude always live successful lives. They embrace the images of possibility, creativity, joyfulness, courage, victory, abundance, peace, success, and happiness.

A traditional Jewish teaching defines winners and losers as follows: winners take to the stage, face up to issues, tread on snow to make a path, govern money, find dreams in their pockets, and never give in to adversity. They do not race for prizes, but find fulfillment in running. Losers, on the other hand, disappear into the crowd, evade issues, wait for the snow to melt, let money govern them, find greed in their pockets, always bemoan adversity, and race for mere prizes without finding fulfillment in the run itself. Their happiness depends on the result of the race.

We need to acknowledge and appreciate the great work God is doing in our lives. With regard to the future, we need to have hope and a vision for what is possible. Never lose sight of the fact that God has absolute dominion over the universe. He is eternal, omnipotent, and faithful.

Such is the Lord God our Father. We are His children, and we must remember that He expects us to be strong and courageous. Be content with what God has given you—your looks, talents, and personality. When you do your best with what you have been given, God will bless you abundantly and your life will be fruitful.

Even withering branches still have a chance to bear fruit as long as they remain on the tree with healthy roots. In much the same way, children of God may be given life and peace as long as they remain in Him.

Negative Attitude

It is not circumstances that make us fail, but a negative attitude towards them. A negative attitude leads us to destruction, leaving behind a sense of failure and defeat. Stay away from people who have a negative attitude. Be careful not to walk in their path, lest they take God's blessing away from you.

Saul's grandson Mephibosheth called himself a "dead dog." Ten of the twelve people Moses sent to explore the land of Canaan likened themselves to grasshoppers. They had a defeatist self-image. A losing mentality is a self-fulfilling reality. Remember that God looks upon us as soldiers.

Positive Attitude

Don't lose sight of the positive attitudes of the great people in the Bible. Joshua and Caleb, those whom Moses sent to explore the land of Canaan, were soldiers whom the Lord was with. Also consider Noah, Ruth, David, Daniel, Job, and other people who found the favor of God in adversity and lived with an attitude of faith. Think of Joseph, who was sold into slavery in Egypt and found the favor of God in adversity. His unwavering trust in God led him to triumph over his sufferings.

When you are at a crossroads and are uncertain what to do, you will do well to seek advice from someone you respect.

Discipline Your Mind

Discouragement, destructive thoughts, fear, anxiety, doubt, restlessness—these do not come from God. They only dissipate our spirit. Don't let such thoughts nest in your mind. Resist them as soon as you sense them creeping in.

The enemy is in your mind, which is why you must turn your attention to God's grace. Look ahead and press on without dwelling on the past. No circumstances, trouble, or adversity fall outside the realm of God. Remember that God is always walking along beside you, especially in times of trouble.

Fix Your Focus

> Finally, brothers, whatever is true, whatever is noble, whatever is right, whatever is pure, whatever is lovely, whatever is admirable—if anything is excellent or praiseworthy—think about such things.
>
> —Philippians 4:8 NIV

When we focus on possibilities from the perspective of God, He will look upon our faith and do amazing things in our lives. Don't let people's demands, pressures, or expectations get in the way of doing what is pleasing to God. Don't deceive yourself by doing what you don't want to do in order not to hurt the feelings of the people who make demands on you. Your life, both at work and at home, must be consistent, for it is seen by your neighbors and friends.

Be glad at all times and think positively. When you do, you will find yourself surrounded by people who are similarly joyful and affirming. Always be humble, while maintaining confidence and self-esteem as a child of God.

Make good use of wisdom, experience, and knowledge, while making plans according to the will of God.

> Trust in the LORD with all your heart and lean not on our own understanding; in all your ways acknowledge him, and he will make your paths straight.
> —Proverbs 3:5-6 NIV

The Lord our God is good, showing us the path ahead and always walking with us.

Chapter 2

CULTIVATE GOOD HABITS

MY BELOVED SON,

Keeping good habits can have a tremendous, positive influence on your life. There is a saying that "the habits you develop as a three-year-old stay with you until you're eighty."

Habits help shape and mold your character more than you may realize. Ultimately, they will determine whether or not you will lead a successful life.

In order to adhere to good principles (honesty, integrity, courage, etc.), it is wise to regulate your daily life by cultivating good habits. Your principles will motivate you to accomplish your goals in life. For example, if you make a promise to someone and make every effort to keep that promise, you will earn that person's respect (and the respect of others who hear of it). Acting on your principles will make you righteous. Straying from them, even not fully cultivating them, will lead only to frustration.

You need to strive to think positively, using the full breadth of your imagination to draw a detailed picture of the meaning of your life.

> Imagination is more important than knowledge, for knowledge is limited while imagination embraces the entire world.
> —Albert Einstein (1879-1955)

It is imagination that gives birth to our dreams and awakens our potential, enabling us to see with our hearts what our eyes cannot. Imagination is the ability to create anything from nothing. And imagination is the wellspring from which flow our hopes and dreams. When you establish a goal for yourself, your imagination will enable you to foresee its outcome before you even set out to accomplish it. In other words, when you feel as though you can't move forward because of fear that you might fail, think positively. Use your imagination to rid yourself of such negativity.

Habit of Reading and Meditating on the Bible

One essential habit you must keep is to read and meditate on the Bible every morning for half an hour. There is no greater wisdom than that which comes from God.

All Scripture is God-breathed and is useful for teaching, rebuking, correcting and training in righteousness.

—2 Timothy 3:16 NIV

The Bible also tells us that the Word of God will bestow wisdom and a peaceful heart, inspiring us to do great things. Also, while you are mediating on God's Word, keep an open heart and mind so that you allow God to speak to you.

Habit of Charity

With the advent of the Internet, the world has become one global society, and we now have a perpetually open window into the lives of our neighbors around the world. The view is not always beautiful—war, poverty, famine, and disease abound. But instead of closing our eyes to the sufferings of the world, we should open our arms to others. Cultivating a love of our fellow man, especially those most in need of help, should be a constant, driving principle, not merely a temporary gesture to make us feel good about ourselves. For instance, you can practice love for your less fortunate neighbors by setting aside a portion of your income each month to donate to charity. Those who receive your charity will be blessed by you, but in cultivating that habit of charity, you also will be blessed by God in knowing that you are doing what is right before Him—that is, obeying Jesus' commandment to love your neighbor as yourself.

Habit of Recording Your Goals

Another good habit to cultivate is writing down your goals and principles and meditating on them. This will connect you with your subconscious mind and help put concrete form to your thoughts. You must do this every day, for the only way to instill good habits is through constant repetition.

The book, *The 7 Habits of Highly Effective People* by Stephen R. Covey, offers insight on the importance of good habits. The seven habits that Covey ascribes to highly effective people are:

1. Being proactive
2. Beginning with the end in mind
3. Putting first things first
4. Thinking win/win (for everyone)
5. Seeking first to understand . . . then to be understood
6. Synergizing (working well in groups)
7. Sharpening the saw (self-renewal)[1]

Habits One, Two, and Three will help you to grow from being dependent to being independent, allowing you to create a strong identity and realize your unique capabilities. Habits Four, Five, and Six will take you from independence to interdependence. With these habits, you can cultivate good relationships, deepen existing relationships, and even heal broken ones.

Habit Seven is the habit of renewal. This habit embodies all the other habits and is therefore essential for continued self-improvement. Self-renewal is the foundation on which further growth and improvement are made. This growth and improvement build character, benefiting both the individual and society.

Good habits form character. They can be developed only through conscious effort and repeated practice because habits are developed through repetition, whether consciously or subconsciously. Therefore, the way to live a bountiful life is through cultivating good habits.

Chapter 3

ALWAYS BE PREPARED

MY BELOVED SON,

In all things, always do your best to be prepared. Whether the task is large or small, when responsibility falls on you, you must be prepared to face it head on. In order to be prepared, you must be qualified for the position you're in so you can live up to your responsibilities. Here are two examples that demonstrate polar opposites of preparedness.

When Hurricane Katrina struck New Orleans in August of 2005, Michael Brown, the director of FEMA (Federal Emergency Management Agency), who was responsible for coordinating the federal government's response to such natural disasters, delayed in sending help to the besieged citizens of New Orleans. His lack of preparedness at such a critical moment caused needless pain and suffering of many citizens.

On the other hand, during the terrorist attack on the World Trade Center on September 11, 2001, and in the days immediately afterward, former New York mayor Rudolph Giuliani showed unwavering leadership in first calming the anxious people of New York and then coordinating New York's response to the tragedy. He truly was well prepared to lead. The difference between being well prepared and unprepared not only affects you, but those around you as well.

These two examples demonstrate how important it is to be well prepared for the unexpected.

Traits of Preparedness

In order to be prepared for whatever life has in store, you must first develop certain traits. Foremost among them are self-confidence and a positive attitude. Avoid complaining or criticizing without presenting an alternative plan or solution. With any situation, do not try to solve the matter impulsively; rather, proceed with caution as you gather and sort the information you'll need to make sound decisions.

Honesty, humility, and tolerance of others are crucial for resolving any matter and are essential for living a prepared life. An arrogant and inconsiderate attitude will not only needlessly disrupt harmony, but it will also create enemies. Whatever the task at hand, setting a goal and proceeding forward in a cautious but decisive manner is the best way to gain the acceptance and respect of others.

A Father's Prayer

Build me a son, O Lord, who will be strong enough to know when he is weak, and brave enough to face himself when he's afraid; one who will be proud of unbending in honest defeat, and humble and gentle in victory.

Build me a son whose wishbone will not be where his backbone should be; a son who will know Thee—and that to know himself is the foundation stone of knowledge. Lead him, I pray, not in the path of ease and comfort, but under the stress and spur of difficulties and challenge. Here let him learn to stand up in the storm; here let him learn compassion for those who fail. Build me a son whose heart will be clear, whose goal will be high; a son who will master himself before he seeks to master other men; one who will learn to laugh, yet never forget how to weep; one who will reach into the future yet never forget the past. After all these things are his, add, I pray, enough of a sense of humor, so that he may not always be serious, yet never take himself too seriously. Give him humility, so that he may always remember the simplicity of true strength. Then, I his father, will dare to whisper, "I have not lived in vain."[2]

—General Douglas MacArthur (1880-1964)

As gold is tested by fire, the true character of a person is revealed through adversity. Toward the end of the American Civil War, on April 9, 1865, in Appomattox, Virginia, the commander of the Union Army, General Ulysses S. Grant, received a surrender notice from the commander of the Confederate Army, General Robert E. Lee.

They had been comrades some twenty years earlier during the Mexican War but had become the leaders of opposing armies during the Civil War. However, because General Grant handled the surrender of the Confederate Army with dignity, these two men were able to end four long years of war.

Even in defeat, General Lee remained a hero to many and General Grant went on to become the eighteenth president of the United States. A person who is understanding and considerate of other people is a *prepared* person.

David was a shepherd until he was twenty years old. His quick mind and fearless spirit were developed as he defended his flock from bears and lions. When David met Goliath in battle after the Philistines invaded Israel, he, no doubt, pictured Goliath as one of the beasts he had fought while guarding his sheep.

David did not possess a coat of armor, but instead he took only his staff and sling. Choosing five smooth stones from a stream, he placed them in his pouch and approached the towering Philistine. As he had done when confronting hungry lions and bears that wanted to make a meal of one of his sheep, David tensed his arm and pulled back his sling, pausing briefly to aim. He then released the stone, which flew straight for Goliath's forehead, killing him instantly.

Even though David was seemingly illprepared to confront his much larger opponent armed with merely a sling, he knew exactly what it would take to fell the giant.

As the story of David and Goliath shows us, we need to be prepared at all times, for nothing happens by chance. If you are always open to learning, you will gradually increase your ability and preparedness to lead. We learn from the great people of the Bible and those throughout history that the way to confront a challenge is with the confidence and courage that come from being well prepared.

See it Through

When you're up against a trouble,
Meet it squarely, face to face;
Lift your chin and set your shoulders,
Plant your feet and take a brace.
When it's vain to try to dodge it,
Do the best that you can do;
You may fail, but you may conquer,
See it through!
Black may be the clouds about you
And your future may seem grim,
But don't let your nerve desert you;
Keep yourself in fighting trim.
If the worst is bound to happen,
Spite of all that you can do,
Running from it will not save you,
See it through!

Even hope may seem but futile,
When with troubles you're beset,
But remember you are facing

Just what other men have met.
You may fail, but fall still fighting;
Don't give up, whate'er you do;
Eyes front, head high to the finish.
See it through![3]

—Edgar A. Guest (1881-1959)

Chapter 4

PAINT A BIG PICTURE

MY BELOVED SON,

Life can be compared to a marathon. However, too many people live as if life is a sprint, acting in impatience and living as if there is no tomorrow. To run well in a marathon requires hard training, patience, and determination.

Those best equipped to excel in the marathon that is life are spiritually strong. In fact, they become stronger as the race wears on and run their fastest as they approach the finish line. With a broader perspective, they are capable of grander visions and goals and therefore paint their lives on a larger canvas. They leave behind past failures, which would only weigh them down, and run freely toward their goal. My son, to paint a bigger picture, you must approach the race with total understanding and with a willingness to lead.

Let's examine some of the qualities of people who paint a bigger picture.

Set Long-Term Goals

First, they set long-term goals, plan, and continually reassess and reevaluate their progress toward achieving their goals.

Exercise Self-Discipline

Second, people painting a big picture possess a high degree of self-discipline. In the book *A Resilient Life*, Gordon MacDonald quotes from another book, *The Perfect Mile,* in which the author, Neil Bascomb, tells the story of the three runners who competed to be the first to break the four-minute mile record:

> All three runners endured thousands of hours of training to shape their bodies and minds. They ran more miles in a year than many of us walk in a lifetime. They spent a large part of their youth struggling for breath. They trained week after week to the point of collapse, all to shave off a second, maybe two, during a mile race—the time it takes to snap one's fingers and register the sound.

> There were sleepless nights and training sessions in rain, sleet, snow and scorching heat. There were times when they wanted to go out for a beer or a date but they knew they couldn't. They understood that life was somehow different for them, that idle happiness eluded them. If they weren't training

or racing or gathering the will required for these efforts, they were trying not to think about training or racing at all.[4]

My son, any goal worth achieving will not come easily. Rather, it will be the fruit of considerable labor, but it will taste so much the sweeter for it.

Train Your Intellect

Third, people painting a big picture train their intellect. The mind is like a muscle—without stimulation it will become weak. With stimulation, however, it becomes stronger. An untrained intellect is lazy and can be easily manipulated by others. However, a well-disciplined intellect is independent and seeks to evaluate and estimate on its own.

A well-disciplined intellect is developed through intensive reading. Books are a bridge to thoughts that have stood the test of time from generation to generation. We build our wisdom from books and learn valuable insight into the human condition. Books are the unseen teacher that helps us develop our powers of critical thinking and self-expression. In assimilating the thought of others, we find our own voice.

I wrote to you earlier about the importance of cultivating good habits. One such habit is reading daily. Especially important is reading from the Bible, which has provided wisdom and guidance to countless souls for two millennia.

Possess an Unyielding Will

Fourth, people painting a big picture possess an unyielding will. No matter what kind of obstacles they face, they never succumb to discouragement. Even if they fall seven times, they will get up each time and continue to strive forward.

Mother to Son

Well, son, I'll tell you;
Life for me ain't been no crystal stair.
It's had tacks in it,
And splinters,
And boards torn up,
And places with no carpet on the floor.
Bare.
But all the time
I'se been a-climbin' on,
And reachin' landin's,
And turnin' corners,
And sometimes goin' in the dark
Where there ain't been no light.
So, boy, don't you turn back.
Don't you set down on the steps.
'Cause you finds it's kinder hard.
Don't you fall now . . .
For I'se still goin', honey,
I'se still climbin'
And life for me ain't been no crystal stair.[5]

—Langston Hughes (1902-1967)

Build Up a Spiritual Environment

Fifth, people painting a big picture know how to build up a spiritual environment. Maintaining a healthy spiritual environment is essential for pursuing your dreams with any conviction.

Life with the Holy Spirit is like a seed—to grow, it must be planted in rich soil. Replacing Sunday worship service with a TV service is very dangerous. With the exception of unavoidable circumstances, Sunday worship service must take place among a community of believers, in a church where God's Spirit resides.

> Swarms of living creatures will live wherever the river flows. There will be large numbers of fish, because this water flows there and makes the salt water fresh; so where the river flows everything will live.
> —Ezekiel 47:9 NIV

That scripture tells us how our sprit revives through the sanctuary. Ignoring the principles of worship will bring confusion and uncertainty.

Also, keeping a prayerful life in an environment where no one else prays can be difficult. To seek God and His kingdom in this material world can be difficult, especially when we socialize with people outside of God's presence. Therefore, to have a good spiritual life, it is important for us to create a spiritually-constructive environment at home or at work. We know that God has given us friends, books, church, the arts, music, and the whole of nature so that through them the seed of faith can grow into a mighty tree. With all we have been given, we should strive to strengthen our spiritual life.

Lastly, I recommend that you read a couple of other books that speak of people who paint a big picture: *A Resilient Life* by Gordon MacDonald mentioned above and *Here and Now* by Henri J. M. Nouwen.[6]

Chapter 5

LEAD
A VICTORIOUS LIFE

MY BELOVED SON,

From the moment they open their eyes each morning, many people begin their day by taking inventory of their problems. If you begin each day overly concerned with the minutiae that makes up so much of daily life, your problems will give you no rest throughout the day.

To develop a broader perspective, start your day with morning devotions (reading from the Bible). You will find the assurance that comes from knowing that our Lord is standing beside you and sharing in your burdens.

Living a Life Spent with God

Leading a victorious life means living a life spent with God. The Old Testament tells us that Daniel lived a victorious life. Even though he was held captive by the Babylonians, he continued to pray to God three times a day, as he had resolved to do. Even though he served the Babylonian king for three years, Daniel didn't defile himself with the royal food and wine. He ate only vegetables and drank water and yet he looked healthier and better nourished than any of the young men who ate the royal food.

Even when he was sent to the lions' den, he trusted the Lord, who made him to see only the angels gathered by his side, not the lions. While Daniel endured much suffering and adversity, he always obeyed God and trusted in God's Word, and so he led a victorious life.

Joseph from the Old Testament was a dreamer. At the age of seventeen, Joseph told his brothers of a dream in which they served him. Later, they sold him into slavery in Egypt. Nevertheless, because of Joseph's trust and faith in God, God was always with him. This was evident to Potiphar, one of Pharaoh's officials, who recognized that God was with Joseph and so trusted him to oversee his estate. Even when Joseph was later unjustly imprisoned after Potiphar's wife falsely accused him of rape, God remained steadfast.

When at age thirty Joseph rose to become second-in-line to the throne of Egypt, Pharaoh knew he couldn't find another man like Joseph—one in whom the Spirit of God rested (Genesis 41:38). Joseph's unwavering trust in God led him to triumph over his sufferings.

In *The Problem of Pain* (1940), the famous author C. S. Lewis (1898-1963) aptly described human suffering.

Pain, in fact, is synonymous with "suffering," "anguish," "tribulation," "adversity," or "trouble," and it is about it that the problem of pain arises. The proper good of a creature is to surrender itself to its creator. When it does so, it is good and happy. The will conferred by the creator is thus perfectly offered back in delighted and delighting obedience by the creature. There, most undoubtedly, is Heaven, and there the Holy Ghost proceeds.

In the world as we now know it, the problem is how to recover this self-surrender. Then, to the question why our cure should be painful, is that to render back the will which we have so long claimed for our own, is in itself, wherever and however it is done, a grievous pain.[7]

Obedience to God

Obedience to God is the only path that leads to a victorious life. Joseph and Daniel triumphed over their adversities because they were faithful and obedient to God even in the midst of their sufferings. While you are unlikely, I pray, to ever face challenges on par with those of Joseph and Daniel, you will no doubt encounter many obstacles and face many challenges as you make your way through this competitive world. Each time you try to solve them in your own way, you will only cause yourself more frustration and agony. Lay everything down before God—all your petty concerns, your deepest anxieties, your minor shortcomings, and your major failings. He will ease your burden and draw you closer to Him.

Trust in God Alone

We need to trust in God alone and not in people. Ask God to make you faithful and obedient. Here is a sample prayer:

> God, make me a blessing to all people I encounter, as Abraham was. Guide me in Your will and widen my boundaries like You did for Jabez. As Agur prayed, ". . . Give me neither poverty nor riches, but give me only my daily bread. Otherwise, I may have too much and disown You and say, 'Who is the LORD?' Or I may become poor and steal, and so dishonor the name of my God."
>
> —Proverbs 30:8-9 NIV

Live by God's Word

> Blessed is the man who does not walk in the counsel of the wicked or stand in the way of sinners or sit in the seat of mockers. But his delight is in the law of the LORD, and on his law he meditates day and night. He is like a tree planted by streams of water, which yields its fruit in season and whose leaf does not wither. Whatever he does prospers.
>
> —Psalm 1:1-3 NIV

My dear son, blessed are those who live by God's Word. Leading a victorious life means obeying God's will for you in any and all circumstances, even when it is at odds with your own will. Just as the tree planted near water is healthy and green and yields fruit, when we trust and obey God, our Lord will lead us to a fruitful and victorious life.

Chapter 6

TEAR DOWN THE TOWER OF BABEL IN YOU

MY BELOVED SON,

Just as our hair will continue to grow and become unmanageable if we don't trim it, so too will our desires grow and become unmanageable if we don't restrain them. Thousands of years ago when God grew weary of the relentlessly sinful nature of man, He chose the one righteous man He could find—Noah, and instructed him to prepare himself and his family for a great flood that would destroy all of mankind. God would then repopulate the human race with descendants of Noah. But as is typical of our sinful nature, mankind eventually strayed from God's will.

> Come, let us build ourselves a city, with a tower that reaches to the heavens, so that we may make a name for ourselves and not be scattered over the face of the whole earth.
>
> —Genesis 11:4 NIV

It was only after God scattered them over all the earth and confused their language that they stopped building the tower, which was called the Tower of Babel.

The pages of the Bible are replete with story after story of men willfully disobeying God and succumbing to the self-centered, sinful aspects of our nature. When we choose to ignore God and follow our own path, we inevitably surrender to arrogance, bitterness, and vengeance, among a host of other negative emotions. Beware, then, for when we first disobey God, we lay the foundation for a Tower of Babel within our hearts.

Once the first brick is laid, it becomes easier to lay the next and easier still after that. Eventually, and often without realizing it, we have built a tower to the heavens—in effect signifying that we are at the same level as God.

Western culture's roots lie in ancient Greece and Rome, whose religions were polytheistic, meaning they worshipped a multitude of gods. The twelve most significant of these were thought to live on Mt. Olympus, the tallest mountain in Greece. The Greeks invested their gods with the same emotions and physical characteristics that they themselves possessed, but only the gods were eternal. Greek mythology became the foundation for Western literature and the visual arts.

When you look at the literature of ancient Greece, one theme appears most often, and that is vengeance. Take, for example, *The Iliad* by Homer (800 B.C.), one of the most famous works in all of literature. The main characters—Achilles, Agamemnon, and Hector—are all consumed with exacting vengeance upon their enemies.

One act of revenge begets another and so on in an endless cycle of violence.

Other great works of literature from ancient Greece are much the same, including *The Odyssey*, again by Homer, the *Oresteia Trilogy* by Aeschylus, *Ajax* by Sophocles, and *Medea* and *Orestes* by Euripides.

From God's point of view, although we were made in His image, our sins separate us from Him. The terrible chasm could only be bridged through the sacrifice of Jesus Christ. Contrary to the famous soliloquy in Shakespeare's *Hamlet* (1601) by Shakespeare (1564-1616), wherein the Prince of Denmark contemplates ending his life and utters the most recognized line in all of literature, "To be or not to be, that is the question," we live and die not by our own choosing but solely through the will of God. When we neglect to make God the center of our lives, which by necessity means that we live first and foremost for ourselves, we invite destruction, for that is what separation from God is—destruction.

Crime and Punishment (1866) and *The Brothers Karamazov* (1879-80) by Fyodor Dostoevsky (1821-81), *The Red and the Black* (1830) by Stendhal (1783-1842), *The Count of Monte Cristo* (1885) by Alexandre Dumas (1802-70), and *An American Tragedy* (1925) by Theodore Dreiser (1871-1945) are all great books, but what else do they have in common? With unmitigated honesty, and regardless of setting or cultural milieu, they depict the universality of man's sinful nature. What these books say is that with all of modern society's technological and scientific advances and increased material wealth, man has marginalized God and made himself the center of the universe.

Despite all we have built, we have destroyed much. Ethics and morality have collapsed. Confusion reigns. Without even realizing it, we have disobeyed God and built a tower of Babel in our hearts. And without God, the pursuit of our dreams and ideals is ultimately meaningless, or as that other great Shakespearean tragic figure Macbeth lamented, it is "a walking shadow . . . full of sound and fury, signifying nothing."

Another theme common to many great works of literature is the search for Utopia—a place of ideal perfection. Such works as *Utopia* (1516) by Thomas More, *The City of the Sun* (1602) by Tommaso Campanella, *New Atlantis* (1627) by Francis Bacon, *Robinson Crusoe* (1719) by Daniel Defoe, *Gulliver's Travels* (1726) by Jonathan Swift, and *Looking Backward* (1888) by Edward Bellamy, depict this desire and search for a perfect world. Of course, Utopia does not exist. Not in this world, anyway. Even if human beings could design and build a Utopia—putting aside our sinful nature, which would render such a task impossible—it would never be more than a Tower of Babel.

Without God as the foundation, anything we build is certain to fall.

> Unless the LORD builds the house, its builders labor in vain. Unless the LORD watches over the city, the watchmen stand guard in vain.
> —Psalm 127:1 NIV

My beloved son, if we do not build our lives upon the foundation of God's Word, our sinful nature will ultimately build a Tower of Babel in our hearts—a tower made not with brick and mortar, but with envy, spite, distrust, greed, pride, and a host of negative emotions that arise when we willfully distance ourselves from our Creator.

It is a constant struggle, but if we live each day guided by the Word of God, we will tear down the Tower of Babel forming in our hearts. This is how we receive new life from the Lord as well as give new life to our neighbors.

> Remain in me, and I will remain in you. No branch can bear fruit by itself; it must remain in the vine. Neither can you bear fruit unless you remain in me.
>
> —John 15:4 NIV

SECTION TWO

BEAUTIFUL PERSON

Chapter 7

ALWAYS GIVE THANKS

MY BELOVED SON,

Give thanks to God for even the smallest thing, for God bestows blessings of joy, peace, and happiness on those with a thankful heart.

However, life without gratitude to God brings anxiety, fear, and dissatisfaction to one's heart. The peace and contentment that comes from a thankful heart was well expressed by a nineteenth century French writer.

> Some people are always grumbling because roses have thorns: I am thankful that thorns have roses.
> —Alphonse Karr (1808-1890)

Your outlook on life will determine whether you have a thankful or a discontented heart. When we give thanks to God, His peaceful and loving presence in our lives becomes almost palpable.

Nicholas Herman (1611-1691), or Brother Lawrence as he came to be known, was a French monk who understood the importance of living in God's presence through daily conversation with Him. Working in the monastery kitchen for fifteen years, he felt the presence of God even while performing the most mundane tasks, such as washing dishes or frying eggs. After his death, his letters and conversations were published as *The Practice of the Presence of God,* in which he explained the simple things we can do in our daily lives to ensure that we live in the presence of God.[8]

As many who have lived a monastic life attest, one sure way to experience the presence of God is through simple chores. Brother Lawrence approached every daily chore with genuine love and obedience in his heart, always striving to make a pure love offering to God. In emulating Brother Lawrence and approaching our mundane tasks with joy, we will find that God's presence is manifest not only in the endless starlit night sky that surrounds the earth, or the vast oceans that cover it, or the majestic mountains that rise from it, but also in the smallest things and in the quietest corners of our lives. Give thanks to God for the littlest things, for in doing so you will live in His presence.

If we can value our most commonplace tasks as given by God and value everyone we meet as a child of God, our anxiety and dissatisfaction will disappear, and in their place we will find a thankful heart. Dietrich Bonhoeffer (1906-1945) was a German theologian who was executed by the Nazis for conspiring in a plot to assassinate Hitler. While imprisoned, Bonhoeffer on occasion received visits from friends. In *Letters and Papers from Prison*, a collection of Bonhoeffer's writing while in prison, he expresses how grateful he was to be able to continue these friendships:

> You see, it would be wrong to suppose that prison life is uninterrupted torture. It certainly is not, and visits like yours relieve it for days on end, even though they do, of course, awaken feelings that have fortunately lain dormant for a while. But that does not matter either. I realize again in thankfulness how well off I was, and feel new hope and energy. Thank you very much, you yourself and the others . . .[9]

We have countless things to be thankful for in our lives, and giving thanks to God means that our existence is no accident. Moreover, it deepens our understanding that we are God's children. Although we cannot foresee our future, if we continually strive to walk daily with God, the burden of anxiety and worries that we shoulder will be light, for God will share in it. Those who live without gratitude to God and who spend their lives complaining about their lives will eventually lose all perspective. They have placed themselves before God and will be consumed by their grievances. Carried too far, complaints and worries can have negative psychological as well as physical affects. Anxiety is like a virus that spreads throughout our being. It carries with it related symptoms such as fear, doubt, frustration, irritation, envy, greed, and depression.

A cheerful heart is good medicine, but a crushed
spirit dries up the bones.

—Proverbs 17:22 NIV

It is foolish to worry about tomorrow if you can't
take care of today. Faith enables us to manage our
troubles and view them with the proper perspective.

Who of you by worrying can add a single hour to
his life?

—Matthew 6:27 NIV

My beloved son,

Let us praise the Lord who came down to earth to
save us.

Let us give thanks to the Lord for strengthening us
when we are weak.

Let us exalt the Lord for always being with us—when
we are downcast, when we are joyful, when we are in
physical or emotional pain, and even when we are
performing the smallest task.

Let us give thanks to the Lord for giving us eternal
life.

Let us confess that the only thing we can give our
Lord is our thankfulness.

Give thanks to the LORD, for he is good; his love
endures forever.

—Psalm 118:1 NIV

Chapter 8

BEAUTIFUL PERSON

MY BELOVED SON,

As long as you live, always try your best to be a beautiful person.

A Beautiful Person Thinks Beautifully

Our thoughts create our future. If we choose to be cheerful, to think positively even when things aren't going well for us, nothing and no one will be able to destroy our positive attitude. There is no arbitrary and inescapable fate that controls our lives. Rather, as Christians who believe in an almighty and loving God, we draw strength, hope, and courage from the belief that our future can change.

Humans have been created to think, and the value
and dignity of humans comes from thinking.

—Blaise Pascal, French philosopher
and mathematician (1623-1662)

Positive thinking is always beautiful. Positive
thoughts are like an inoculation protecting us against
the negativity that we are susceptible to when we are
pressured by hardships and adverse circumstances.

In an Old Testament story in the book of Numbers,
Joshua and Caleb had been sent to spy on the rival
Canaanite encampment and reported back to the Israelite
assembly that even though the Israelites were outnumbered, still they would swallow up the Canaanites, for
the Lord was with them. Joshua and Caleb understood
that with God, nothing is impossible. By contrast, the
other ten spies who had accompanied Joshua and Caleb
were wrought with fear and compared the Canaanites
to giants and the Israelites to grasshoppers. Ultimately,
the unfailing faith of Joshua and Caleb was rewarded, as
they were the only two of the twelve spies to eventually
make it to the Promised Land.

A thoughtful person is one who seeks wisdom,
which comes from God and is like pure spring water
that rises from deep within the forest, transcending our
own limited knowledge and understanding. To grow
spiritually we need to meditate on and live by God's
Word daily. Doing so roots us in the Word of God and
gives us wisdom and understanding.

Proverbs 30:24-28 describes four of the smallest
things on earth that make up in wisdom what they lack

in size. They are ants of little strength, yet they store up food in the summer; creatures of little power, yet they make a home in the crags; locusts without a king, yet they advance together in ranks; and lizards that can be caught with the hand, yet are found in the palaces of kings. These passages teach us that to develop wisdom we must learn from the smallest things on earth. As iron sharpens iron, if you surround yourself with wise people, you will become wiser.

> By wisdom a house is built, and through understanding it is established; through knowledge its rooms are filled with rare and beautiful treasures.
>
> —Proverbs 24:3-4 NIV

A Beautiful Person Speaks Beautifully

Words are powerful. They can both save life as well as take life. They can give expression to our hopes and dreams and to our frustration and despair. Some people use their words like whips and swords to complain and gossip, while others use their words like open arms that welcome a friend and express gratitude, love, and encouragement.

Christopher Reeve (1952-2004) was an actor who became famous for playing Superman in several films in the 1970s and 1980s. He was so associated with the role that "Superman" became his nickname. As you probably know, Reeve was tragically paralyzed in a horse riding accident in 1995.

The character of Superman is a selfless hero who fights for those who can't fend for themselves. After

Reeve became paralyzed, he was the one who needed help. He could no longer chew and swallow food, nor go to bathroom on his own. Just to breathe air into his lungs required the aid of an oxygen tank.

Distraught with feelings of helplessness, his first thought upon realizing his predicament was that it would be better for everyone if he were to die. He told his doctor that he wanted to end his life. Of course, the doctor told him that he would need his wife's consent. Reeve begged his wife, Dana, to remove his oxygen mask and turn off the tank that pumped oxygen into his lungs and kept him alive. However, Dana whispered to her husband, "You're still you. And I love you. You are conscious and your brain is functioning well. So please just stay alive!"

Dana's words rejuvenated her husband's spirit and restored his will to live. From then on he became determined not only to regain the ability to walk, but to show others by example that *Nothing is Impossible*—the title of his second book. Furthermore, he established the Christopher Reeve Foundation (since renamed the Christopher and Dana Reeve Foundation), a nonprofit organization that funds research for spinal nerve regeneration. Until his death in 2004, he served as a fervent public advocate for people with spinal cord injuries, becoming a true hero and a super man.

Life's Mirror

There are souls that are pure and true,
Then give the world the best you have,
And the best will come back to you.

Give love, and love to your life will flow,
A strength in your utmost need,
Have faith, and a score of hearts will show
Their faith in your word and deed...
For life is the mirror of king and slave,
'Tis just what we are and do;[10]
Then give to the world the best you have,
And the best will come back to you.

—Madeline Bridges (1844-1920)[10]

As the example of Dana Reeves shows, words literally have the power of life—the power to give another human being hope and encouragement. God created the world with His Word, and God's Word is life, power, and love. As God's people, our words possess the power to heal, to give comfort, and to restore hope. Our words can be an expression of God's love. Those who speak words of faith and hope, healing and gratitude, encouragement and love are truly beautiful people.

> The good man brings good things out of the good stored up in his heart, and the evil man brings evil things out of the evil stored up in his heart. For out of the overflow of his heart his mouth speaks.
>
> —Luke 6:45 NIV

A Beautiful Person Lives as a Servant

A selfish person's life is like a thistly thorn bush around which nothing can grow. The life of a selfless person who serves others is like fertile soil that yields a rich harvest. Serving others is not easy. It requires sacrifice, dedication, and humility, but, like anything so demanding, the outcome is well worth the effort.

I have been blessed to know many people living beautifully in their service to the church, their fellow Christians, and neighbors. They serve quietly and with humble obedience whenever and wherever they are needed. No matter how busy their schedules, they always make time to volunteer. I have watched them place the needs of others before their own even when they had every reason to be preoccupied with their own lives. Their profound faith is like a quiet, but mighty river strong enough to carry a heavy weight and steady enough to help people reach their destination. I am humbled by such selfless people and marvel at how they stand firm, resolute in living a life of sacrifice as Jesus taught us.

> The Son of Man did not come to be served, but to serve, and to give his life as a ransom for many.
> —Matthew 20:28 NIV

A Beautiful Person Gives Thanks and Praise

The light that emanates from a joyful soul in the midst of praise is as bright as morning sunshine.

> Shout for joy to the LORD, all the earth. Worship the LORD with gladness; come before him with joyful songs. Know that the LORD is God. It is he who made us, and we are his; we are his people, the sheep of his pasture. Enter his gates with thanksgiving and

his courts with praise; give thanks to him and praise
his name.

—Psalm 100:1-4 NIV

When we praise the Lord who created us and
sustains us, He pours out His grace upon us until we
are overflowing with joy and peace. Even in the midst of
sorrow, suffering, and despair, we should praise our Lord
with gratitude because His mercy and love are eternal.
The most beautiful things in the world still cannot
compare to the beauty of a soul praising God.

I Love All Beauteous Things

I love all beauteous things.
I seek and adore them;
God hath no better praise.
And man in his hasty days
is honored for them.

I too will something make
And joy in the making!
Altho' tomorrow it seem'
Like the empty words of a dream
Remembered, on waking.[11]

—Robert Bridges (1844-1930)

A Beautiful Person is Always Prepared

We never know when the Lord will call us, nor when
He will return. Whether it will be day or night, we do

not know. In the book of Matthew, Jesus explains that
the kingdom of heaven is like a wedding banquet where
ten virgins wait for the bridegroom.

> Five of them were foolish and five were wise. The
> foolish ones took their lamps but did not take any
> oil with them. The wise, however, took oil in jars
> along with their lamps.
> —Matthew 25:2-4 NIV

When the call went out at midnight that the groom,
who had been delayed, was on his way, the foolish
virgins asked the wise for some oil to light their lamps
so they could go out and meet him. Fearing there
would not be enough oil to go around, the wise virgins
refused and told the foolish virgins to go purchase their
own oil. While they were doing so, the groom arrived
and the wise virgins accompanied him to the banquet
hall. When the foolish virgins returned from buying
oil, they found the doors to the banquet hall closed.
Despite their pleading, the bridegroom claimed that
he did not know them.

> Therefore keep watch, because you do not know the
> day or the hour.
> —Matthew 25:13 NIV

Similarly, Jesus warned of the wealthy but foolish
farmer who stockpiled his bountiful harvest with the
intent of taking life easy and living only for his own
happiness.

But God said to him, "You fool! This very night your
life will be demanded from you. Then who will get
what you have prepared for yourself?

—Luke 12:20 NIV

God was not pleased with this man.

My beloved son, let's put our hope in heaven and be
prepared for the unexpected. We can learn from those
who have gone before us. Their dedication to serving
others and praising God can continue to remind us of
what it means to be a beautiful person. Like them, make
this world an extension of God's kingdom, a place where
we serve others and offer praise and thanks to God with
a beautiful heart.

Chapter 9

HUMBLE UNDER GOD'S MIGHTY HAND

MY BELOVED SON,

No matter how much we strive to feel complete, life in this imperfect world will always leave us feeling that something is lacking because our final destination is eternal life with our Father in heaven. However, too often, in pride and shortsightedness, thinking we will be on this earth forever, we turn away from God.

It is human nature to seek first our own happiness, from which flows the arrogant belief that everything we possess is ours, even things that do not belong to us. Only when we humble ourselves before God do we learn what it means to live a fruitful life. Such humility before God is the only way to live wisely.

An Unfinished Work

Whenever I listen to Schubert's "Unfinished Symphony," I learn the wisdom of humility. I also shared this in my book *Manhattan: Land of Opportunity* (1996).

At age twenty-five, Schubert composed *Unfinished Symphony* No. 8 in B minor. Typically, a symphony has four movements, but *Unfinished* contains only two. It is literally an unfinished symphony. However, Schubert's *Unfinished Symphony* has been loved by music lovers from all over the world, as much as Beethoven's *Symphony* No. 5 in B minor *Op. 67*, Tchaikovsky's *Symphony* No. 6 in B minor, *Op.74 Pathetique*, and Berlioz's *Symphony Fantastique*.

Schubert was one of the most brilliant composers of the Romantic Period. His "Unfinished Symphony" has such a beautiful and rich melody, and his use of harmony is excellent as well. Often when I listen to it, I wonder why it is as lauded by musicians and critics alike when it is so much shorter than most other symphonies. Could it be that the form itself is incomplete, but the content is complete? Or is there an implicit beauty in the very nature of incompleteness? Perhaps its mysterious melody, which seems to be carried by the wind as it softly reaches our ears, is what so leaves an impression on us.

Not being a professional musician or music critic, it is hard for me to understand in musical terms why "Unfinished Symphony" is so highly praised. However, whenever I listen to it I am reminded that no matter how long we live on this earth, life is unfinished. We will only find completion with God in heaven. Life on earth is like a journey, for in a little while we need to return to our Father's house in heaven.

When we are young we feel as though we will live forever. As we grow older we feel the passing of time more acutely and realize how short life really is. With the horizon seemingly so far in the distance, we occupy the empty spaces of our lives with activities that keep us from dwelling on the inevitability of death. But no matter how hard we try to fill the empty spaces of life, they can never be filled. Death compels us to be honest with ourselves, which is why some people are filled with regret as they confront death and acutely feel the incompleteness of their lives.

I have often felt that something was lacking in my life. I sometimes have feelings of emptiness, which may be why I enjoy listening to Schubert's "Unfinished Symphony." And maybe my own view differs from that of professional musicians and music critics, but in my opinion, the power of "Unfinished Symphony" comes from its incompleteness. Schubert's symphony reminds us of our insufficiency. This mystical power that is common to all great works of art is like a mirror in which we see our shortcomings, and before which we acquire humility.

We possess an endless yearning to be the center of attention. It is part of our nature to want to be looked upon favorably by others. However, Schubert's "Unfinished Symphony" teaches us how to control this desire. Wisdom lies in acknowledging that we are imperfect; that our earthly life is by its very nature incomplete, and that because of this we ought to live with humility.

In order to remain humble, we must guard against falling under the spell of flattery and personal recognition, which play so strongly into our desire to be known and liked by others. Unless we are cautious and train ourselves with disciplined humility, our desire to be recognized will tempt us to succumb to our pride, which always lurks just beneath the surface.

Follow the Best Examples

At the same time, there have been notable public figures who set an excellent example of humility for us to follow. One such person is Jimmy Carter, a former president of the United States, who has done and continues to do charitable work through Habitat for Humanity. Another is Albert Schweitzer (1875-1965), who was equally trained as a musician, theologian, and physician and devoted much of his life to serving the poor in the West African nation of Gabon. Then there is Mother Teresa (1910-1997), who devoted her life to the poor and neglected people of Calcutta, India.

These three people followed the example of the Son of God, who came down to earth to serve the weak, the poor, and the neglected. Why would Christ give up glory in heaven to come to earth as a servant, lowering himself to the point of dying on the cross? Because God raises up and those who humbly serve others.

> Humble yourselves, therefore, under God's mighty hand, that he may lift you up in due time.
>
> —1 Peter 5:6 NIV

Chapter 10

FOR YOUR LONELY NEIGHBOR

MY BELOVED SON,

If we look around at our neighbors, we find some who are at peace, fully aware of the love God has for them and who therefore can live a life of love for their fellow man and thanksgiving to God. On the other hand, we see people suffering with loneliness and depression, who feel a palpable emptiness that leaves them bereft of hope for the future. Under great emotional duress, this intense sadness may lead them to succumb to their despair and take their own lives.

One person's life is more precious than the entire world. Remember the parable of the lost sheep, in which the shepherd gladly leaves his entire flock in the open country to recover the one sheep that has strayed from the flock (Luke 15:3-7).

Similarly, show your love for your troubled neighbor by listening to him or her and offering comfort if you can. Even if you are busy with work, still, make yourself available.

When you are talking to people, your focus should be on their salvation. You will be surprised how people who live without God try to find the answers to their problems within themselves. Life without God has hardened their unbelief, making it difficult for them to accept God's love or even believe that He exists. However, it is foolish to even think we can live without the Creator, the one responsible for giving us life.

In his book *Pensees*, Blaise Pascal writes with his customary incisive wit that he wants to "contemplate the greatness and the misery of man."

> It is vain that you seek within yourselves the cure for your miseries. All your intelligence can only bring you to realize that it is not within yourselves that you will find either truth or good. The philosophers made such promises and they have failed to keep them. They do not know what your true good is, not what your true state is.

> Your chief maladies are the pride that withdraws you from God, and the lust that binds you to the earth; all they have done is to keep at least one of these maladies going. If they gave you God as an object of study, it was only to exercise your pride.[12]

Life apart from God is lonely and dark. We must therefore remember that it is through our relationship with God that the achievement of our goals derives significance. Even though we dedicate our time, talent, and mental and physical energy to achieving our goals, if our focus is not on God, our lives will be lonely and empty.

Never forget God's amazing love; that He sent His Son to die on the cross for us, though we were undeserving of His love and mercy. We are foolish if we do not acknowledge the continual blessings we receive from God—the talents, the people, and the love that make all of our achievements possible.

It is all too true that when everything goes well in our lives, we become first lazy, neglecting to acknowledge His blessings, and then proud, as we attribute our successes solely to our own effort. But when faced with inevitable sufferings and hardships that remind us of the ephemeral nature of both our achievements and life itself, we quickly turn to God for comfort.

How fortunate we are and how grateful we ought to be, then, that God welcomes us back with open arms like the prodigal children we are. Do not be like those who are too proud to reconcile with God and who end up bringing destruction upon themselves for their arrogance.

Finally, one last thing I'd like to mention as far as being a source of spiritual light for your neighbor is that we could all do with more rest, both for our bodies and our souls. Living like a machine without proper rest dehydrates the spirit. We need to come to God and lay everything down before Him, for in Him we will be renewed.

Learn to Rest So Your Life Will Be Blest

We all need "short vacations"
In life's fast and maddening race—
An interlude of quietness
Form the constant, jet-age pace . . .
So, when your day is pressure packed
And your hours are all too few,
Just close your eyes and meditate
And let God talk to you.
For, when we keep on pushing,
we're not following in God's way—
We are foolish, selfish robots
Mechanized to fill each day
With unimportant trivia
That makes life more complex
And gives us greater problems
to irritate and vex . . .
So, when your nervous network
Becomes a tangled mess,
Just close your eyes in silent prayer
And ask the Lord to bless.

Each thought that you are thinking,
Each decision you must make,
As well as every word you speak
And every step you take,
For only by the grace of God

Can we gain self-control
And only meditative thoughts
Can restore your "peace of soul."[13]

—Helen Steiner Rice (1900-1981)

We need to rest our spirit so that we may find peace
through God's grace and fulfill our mission of delivering
the good news of God's love to our lonely neighbors.

Chapter 11

PRAY
AS YOU GET BUSIER

MY BELOVED SON,

As your life gets busier, you must continue to make time to pray. Prayer is the only way for us to maintain a close relationship with God. As Christians, we must have absolute faith that our Lord Father in heaven listens to and answers our prayers. He answers them at the appropriate time, which doesn't necessarily coincide with our time preferences.

It is through prayer that we grow spiritually. Daily prayer is like breathing for the soul. It should be done regularly every day and not only when we feel the need. Prayer is powerful, and through that power we can experience God's miracles.

I can assure you that once your soul has been trained through continual prayer, you will see firsthand as God works unexpected wonders in your life. As water evaporates and forms clouds, which fill with moisture that is released as rain, so as we continually pray, our prayers will be stored in heaven until God answers them in His own way.

While it is important to establish a regular habit of prayer, it is also important to understand that there is no problem and no circumstance too great for God. What seems impossible to us with our limited perspective is possible for God who is all knowing and all powerful. The power of prayer is within prayer itself, for healing begins with the very act of prayer. When we lay down all of our weakness, pain, and suffering before God, our soul is connected with God, which is how healing occurs. And a person who prays habitually will gain gifts of spiritual power and authority from God. Christian author Richard Foster sums it up in his book *Prayer*.

> We do not leap into the dizzy heights of constant communion in a single bound. It comes over a period of time in measured practical steps. The first step is that of outward discipline. This is how we gain proficiency at anything. The second step is for this work to move into the subconscious mind. We say our prayer, and we are unaware of having said it. The third step occurs as prayer moves into the heart. In reality we are moving with the mind into the heart. The fourth step comes as prayer permeates the whole personality. It becomes like our breath or our blood, which moves through out the entire body. Prayer develops a deep rhythm inside us.[14]

My beloved son, I encourage you to memorize the following verses:

> For the word of God is living and active. Sharper than any double-edged sword, it penetrates even to dividing soul and spirit, joints and marrow; it judges the thoughts and attitudes of the heart. Nothing in all creation is hidden from God's sight. Everything is uncovered and laid bare before the eyes of him to whom we must give account.
>
> —Hebrews 4:12-13 NIV

> Be self-controlled and alert. Your enemy the devil prowls around like a roaring lion looking for someone to devour. Resist him, standing firm in the faith, because you know that your brothers throughout the world are undergoing the same kind of sufferings.
>
> —1 Peter 5:8-9 NIV

Abraham Lincoln (1809-1865), the sixteenth president of the United States, was a man of prayer, who prayed all the more the busier he became. As president in a time of civil war, with so many momentous issues to grapple with, he trusted not in his own judgment, but in God's.

Despite severe setbacks in the first two years of the war, Lincoln never lost faith in the justness of the Union cause or in God. I think the primary reason for the Union's eventual triumph was not due to superiority of combat strength, but rather to Lincoln's ardent belief that slavery was unjust, as well as his unwavering trust in God.

According to history records, early in the Civil War there were not enough Union commanders and the soldiers were often undisciplined, which allowed the Confederates to advance close to Washington, DC. That raised the possibility that the war would end early and disastrously for the Union. At this critical juncture, President Lincoln sought God's help and wisdom. He wanted only one thing—to be pleasing to God—which is, in fact, everything. Like King David, Lincoln was not concerned with whether God was on his side, but whether he (and the Union) were on God's side.

My beloved son, prayer is the spiritual pathway that leads to God. So continue to pray as your life gets busier, for God wants us to draw close to Him. And do not doubt that God will respond to your prayers, for He has said,

> Call to me and I will answer you and tell you great and unsearchable things you do not know.
> —Jeremiah 33:3 NIV

Chapter 12

OVERCOME TRIALS

MY BELOVED SON,

Trials and tribulations are inevitable, and they break on the shores of our lives in waves both small and large. Often they can be caused by those close to us, such as coworkers, friends, and family members. They can be calculated to cause us harm, such as with rumors, or they can be the result of arbitrary circumstances, such as the loss of a job or the death of a loved one. Of course, our own wants and desires can also put us to the test.

When you are faced with a trial of any kind, do not think of it as meaningless suffering.

> When one door is closed, another opens; but we often look so long and so regretfully upon the closed door that we do not see the one which has opened for us.
>
> —Alexander Graham Bell,
> inventor of the telephone (1847-1922)

God allows us to undergo trials so that we can mature, which means that every trial is an opportunity to grow spiritually. Through trials we learn valuable lessons. For example, we learn honesty by overcoming deceitfulness, humility through overcoming arrogance, and perseverance through overcoming the desire to quit when the going gets tough. Success is born from adversity.

Trials also bring with them added temptations.

Four Stages of Temptation

Let's think about how Satan tempts us.

Desire

First, Satan plants the seed of desire in our hearts, where unless we make a conscious effort to rid ourselves of it, it silently and slowly grows like a weed and chokes virtue. In particular, beware of easy shortcuts, which may be Satan's temptation.

Doubt

The second stage is doubt. Satan causes us to doubt what God's Word says in regard to sin. Furthermore, he puts negative thoughts and emotions, such as jealousy and arrogance, into our hearts, which create anxiety and suspicion of everything God has given to us.

Deception

The third stage is deception. Satan whispers lies into our ears, disguising them to make them seem as if they are from God. For example, despite knowing the importance of honesty, we may think that in certain situations speaking honestly would cause more harm than good.

Disobedience

The fourth stage is disobedience. In his deceitfulness, Satan leads our thoughts away from the will of God. As a result, we end up disobeying God and we fall into a snare that Satan has laid.

If we fall into the traps Satan has laid and succumb to his temptations, for a brief period of time we might receive enjoyment and pleasure. However, soon that pleasure and enjoyment will turn into suffering and sorrow.

Resisting and Overcoming Temptation

You can't fight an enemy you don't know even exists.

Awareness

If we are aware of the four stages of temptation and identify them early enough, we will be well prepared to conquer them. Perhaps the best way to overcome temptation is by blocking it from ever entering our hearts.

Alertness

Temptations are so powerful because they bring immediate pleasure. In succumbing to these impulsive pleasures, we then find ourselves doing things we know are wrong in order to cover up our behavior or continue it. That's why it's so important to defeat temptation early on, before it takes hold of us and leads us to do things we know are wrong. The more time we spend grappling with temptation, the weaker our resistance to it becomes and the stronger Satan's temptations grow, bringing ever-greater suffering into our lives.

I'll give you an example of how temptations lead to trials. A friend of mine faced the biggest trial of his life because he couldn't resist alcohol. He enjoyed drinking and never said no when alcohol was offered. He attended a party one evening at which there were plenty of mixed drinks and wines being served, but having driven to the party by himself, he was determined not to drink that night. However, as the party wore on and he saw other party guests drinking and enjoying themselves, he gave in to temptation and had first one drink, and then another, and another until he was totally drunk when the party broke up.

Driving home under the influence of alcohol, he caused a multiple-car accident on the highway and lost consciousness. He awoke the next day in the emergency room and was fortunate to find that he had suffered only minor injuries. His injuries were just the beginning, however, for the repercussions of this accident extended far beyond his physical injuries to wreak havoc emotionally and financially on himself, his family, and his friends.

First, he had wrecked his car beyond repair and had his license suspended, which required him to take public transportation to his job in Manhattan. He lost the respect of his coworkers and was branded as unreliable. He was required to undergo counseling fourteen times for his alcohol addiction and to submit a certificate of completion to the court. After that he went through DDP (Drinking Driver Program) training from the state every Saturday morning for seven weeks. Only after completing those programs did he regain his license to drive.

He has stopped drinking altogether. Learning self-control was a costly lesson for him, but he considers himself fortunate that it didn't cost him his life. In fact, it is miracle that he survived.

Another example: I once had a business acquaintance whom I met a few times each year. One time I met him in Las Vegas—the host city for an annual trade convention at which he always bought new merchandise for his business. To pass the time one evening, he went to a casino to do a little gambling. He quickly got hooked on the games and lost all the money he had with him. Back home, he became obsessed with recouping the money he had lost in Las Vegas. He took to gambling at casinos on a regular basis, abandoning his responsibilities to his family and his business. Ultimately, he lost his family and his fortune.

My beloved son, remember to be on guard at all times against the temptations that lie in wait to seduce and destroy us.

Examination

Examine common characteristics of a trial so you are better prepared to identify and thus avoid temptation before it is too late. Ask yourself these questions:

When am I most susceptible to temptation?

Who stood by me when I faced my toughest trials?

What types of situations are likely to get me into trouble?

Recognize Your Emotional State

There are certain emotional states that make us vulnerable to temptation. When we are tired, lonely, bored, depressed, stressed, hurt, angry, or anxious, we are more likely to sin. But it's not only negative emotions that lead us to temptation—positive emotions can be just as deceiving, such as pride in our accomplishments or even the joy of spiritual uplift. The sooner we can identify the emotions that leave us vulnerable to temptation, the better we'll be able to resist, or better yet, avoid it.

Resist Fear

When we face a trial, we face fear and we mustn't succumb to it.

> Fear is like fire: if controlled, it will help you; if uncontrolled, it will rise up and destroy you"
> —John F. Milburn (1880-1951)

It is inevitable that we will face numerous trials in a world so rife with temptation, but when we do we must confront them courageously.

So, if you think you are standing firm, be careful that you don't fall! No temptation has seized you except what is common to man. And God is faithful; he will not let you be tempted beyond what you can bear. But when you are tempted, he will also provide a way out so that you can stand up under it.

—1 Corinthians 10:12-13, NIV

Rid Yourself of Bad Habits

This is no easy task, for it requires acting against your desires. You need to overcome your lesser bad habits and the smaller trials they entail before overcoming your more severe habits and correspondingly tougher trials. When you feel the impulse of a bad habit, fight it before it takes hold of you and grows into a bigger problem.

Seek God's Help

Understand that God is always waiting for us to call upon Him. Ask God for His help.

Yield Not to Temptation

Yield not to temptation for yielding is sin,
Each victory will help you some other to win;
Fight manfully onward, dark passions subdue,
Look ever to Jesus, He'll carry you through.
Ask the Savior to help you, comfort,
strengthen, and keep you;
He is willing to aid you, He will carry you through.

—Horatio R. Palmer (1834-1907)

God helps those who seek His grace by creating the conditions that enable us to defeat temptation. Since He is waiting to help us, we should not be too proud to seek His help. Often we think we know what's best for us, even more so than God, which prevents us from seeking His help and paves the way to failure. If we honestly examine our lives, we will probably see that we fall into habits or patterns that create the condition for temptations to flourish. And more likely than not, it is the same temptation that plagues us again and again. That's all the more reason to seek God's help.

Trials and hardships can be good for us. They can wake us up to the fact that life is fleeting and that all that we build, believe, and achieve on this earth will not last forever.

Overcoming trials can also teach us valuable lessons. If despite our good intentions, others misjudge our actions as wicked, we can learn humility and forgiveness, as we seek God's help to make things right with our neighbor. In fact, the most important element involved in persevering through and overcoming trials is to stand firm in our faith and to rely on God.

I recommend that you read *Of the Imitation of Christ* by Thomas à Kempis (1380-1471) for additional insights on how to overcome trials.[15] Also, *The Purpose Driven Life* by Rick Warren.[16]

Good books are like unseen teachers, imparting lessons that you can draw on in times of trouble. As you confront the trials that you will inevitably face, I pray that you will win out over temptation, and that in doing so, your faith will deepen.

SECTION THREE
TRUE NEIGHBOR

Chapter 13

AUTUMN LETTER

MY BELOVED SON,

Some people are blessed to live happy and fruitful lives, while others suffer with bitterness, loneliness, and alienation. The season of autumn seems to capture this duality: the bountiful harvest of autumn represents the richness of life, but it also portends that winter is fast approaching. For me, autumn is a time of reflection, a time to think of friends and neighbors. It is a time to write a letter to a dear friend or maybe even to someone you'd like to know better.

Flower

Until I spoke his name,
he had been
no more than a mere gesture.

When I spoke his name,
he came to me
and became a flower.

Now speak my name,
one fitting this color and order of mine,
as I spoke his name,
so that I may go to him
and become his flower.

We all wish
To become something.
You to me and I to you
Wish to become an unforgettable gaze.[17]

—Ch'un-Su Kim

"You to me" or "I to you," we all need to be loved; "to become an unforgettable gaze" to another. Whether joyful or sad, lonely or gregarious, we need someone with whom we can share our emotions . . . our lives. I hope you find that someone to become your "flower" and that you will be hers.

You may know someone who is going through the pain and suffering of a failed romance—someone who would likely welcome the support and encouragement that you could offer. For it seems that to be human is to seek fulfillment in another, which may be why the end of a relationship leaves us feeling empty.

If you think that a letter would provide comfort and encouragement to someone suffering from heartache and loneliness, do not hesitate to write it. If you are the one whose soul is exhausted, I urge you to heed this advice: When you fail in any given situation, be it a relationship or otherwise, do not give up. As a tree that grows through weeds grows stronger and taller, and as a bird that has been in the nest for a long time can fly higher and see farther, you will grow stronger and wiser for persevering through the difficult times of your life.

Whenever I watch the autumn leaves fall, I remember that the Lord said "and the dust returns to the ground it came from, and the spirit returns to God who gave it" (Ecclesiastes 12:7). Before the next autumn fades into winter, listen to what your spirit is singing and spread the message of Ecclesiastes.

I also continually turn to Mother Teresa's writings:

> There is much suffering in the world—very much. Material suffering from hunger, suffering from homelessness, from all kinds of disease, but I still think that the greatest suffering is being lonely, feeling unloved, just having no one. I have come more and more to realize that it is being unwanted that is the worst disease that any human being can ever experience.

> In these times of development, the whole world runs and is hurried. But there are some who fall down on the way and have no strength to go ahead. These are the ones we must care about. Let us be very sincere in our dealings with each other and have the courage to accept each other as we are. Do not be surprised at or become preoccupied with each other's failure.[18]

Yes, the greatest suffering in the world is the numbing loneliness of feeling unloved. In the story *What People are Living By*, Tolstoy (1828-1910) writes, "For all the people, to live life is not just thinking and worrying about oneself, it is to live together with other people."

I encourage you to share a warm heart of love with everyone you know who is suffering from loneliness. Write them a letter that gives them hope, courage, and comfort—there is no greater gift you can give. And in doing so, you will reap a harvest of love from your heavenly Father.

Chapter 14

TRUE NEIGHBOR

MY BELOVED SON,

Let's think about who our true neighbors are.

Who is Our Neighbor?

The entire world was shocked by the terrorist attacks of September 11, 2001 (9/11), and in particular the collapse of the World Trade Center towers in New York. The tragedy that befell New York that day hurled America into one of the biggest crises in the nation's history. The entire nation, and most of the world, mourned for the nearly three thousand innocent victims of these attacks.

As shocking and as tragic as the attacks were, Americans displayed their dignity by standing strong and coming together as one. Think of the fearless firefighters who ran into the burning towers as thousands fled for their lives. These men ascended flight after flight of stairs in their heavy uniforms and with the added weight of oxygen tanks, axes, and sundry firefighting equipment. What enabled these men to be so brave? So many of these brave firefighters lost their lives when the unimaginable happened and the towers collapsed. These men gave their lives to rescue complete strangers, personifying the sacrificial nature of the love of neighbor to which God calls us.

Behavior of a True Neighbor

Remember, too, the spontaneous generosity of people lined up outside hospitals waiting to donate blood and the selfless volunteers who flocked to lower Manhattan in the days after the tragedy to dig for survivors. On street corners and in parks throughout New York City, people gathered to post photos of missing loved ones, and strangers comforted strangers, lighting candles and joining together in shared sorrow. Ironically, the city was never more united than in the aftermath of 9/11, which was evident in the banners and signs held aloft and the chants of "United We Stand" that greeted the convoy of volunteer cleanup workers driving down the West Side Highway to Ground Zero. It was this spontaneous outpouring of love, humanity, and generosity that enabled the wounded citizens of New York and the United States to overcome their time of national crisis.

In the wake of 9/11, people's hearts were filled with the American ideals of freedom, justice, and democracy. From generation to generation, Americans pass down their democratic ideals, the support and defense of which is the foundation of true patriotism. Seemingly overnight, American flags sprouted like flowers from front porches and car windows. In America's response to 9/11, I witnessed the core values that make America so strong—the willingness of its people to rally together despite all their differences.

America, may God bless you and protect you!

Selflessness

As I watched Americans place their concern for their neighbor and their country ahead of their own, I had to ask myself two questions: (1) What kind of person am I to my neighbor? (2) Who is my true neighbor? I felt ashamed that I even had to ask. The answer, of course, is that the true neighbor is the one who can share the pain and suffering of his fellow man.

Too often we think that loving our neighbor entails only talking to him or her. Without even considering whether it is appropriate or desired, we offer our advice and instruct our neighbor without listening. Like a trifoliate orange tree, our words can be thorns that bring pain rather than comfort.

Love Your Neighbor

Until you get to know someone well enough,
Don't be so quick to teach—
That person may know more than you

Don't be so quick to give advice—
That person may have deeper scars than you

Don't be so quick to give and share—
That person may have much to give you

In everything, slow down
Don't rush ahead to help
Follow humbly behind
And lift them up to the Lord

Then and only then
God will show you what you can do

Do as God has shown
Then your heart will know
This is love. [19]

—Young Ja Kim

When it comes to loving our neighbor, we need to learn patience. Don't be so quick to offer your opinion unless it is sought. Allow God to guide your relationship with your neighbor.

The Good Samaritan

The Bible tells us what it means to be a true neighbor through the story of the good Samaritan. The story tells of a Jewish man making his way from Jerusalem to Jericho when he is brutally attacked and left for dead by a robber. A priest and a Levite pass him by without offering to help, but a Samaritan, a member of a group who were adversaries of the Jews, had compassion for him and took care of him. In examining my own life,

I am ashamed at how often I have acted like the priest and the Levite.

Lim Sang Ok

During the Chosun Dynasty in Korea, a very wealthy merchant named Lim Sang Ok (1779-1855), said, "It is better to leave good fortune behind than to leave good people behind." He always considered others before himself and was regarded as a great leader by his fellow merchants. When the economy was doing poorly and the people suffered, he donated much of his wealth to charity. Lim believed that money, like water, should be level among all people; that a righteous person should be like an even scale, treating all people equally.

American Business Titans

In the nineteenth century, America produced a number of business titans in various industries: John Wanamaker (1838-1922) with department stores, Andrew Carnegie (1835-1919) in the steel industry, and John D. Rockefeller (1839-1937) with coal mining.

As well as being captains of industry, these men were great philanthropists, who used their wealth to benefit society in many fields, such as politics, religion, science, literature, philosophy, medicine, and education. What truly made these men great was not their wealth but what they did with it, using it for the betterment of their fellow man.

Seagulls

If you ever observe seagulls in flight, you will notice right away that they form a "V." In this way, seagulls can fly up to seventy percent farther than if they flew in single file. Flying together as one makes it easier on all of them, enabling them to cover greater distances than they could individually. Similarly, we can accomplish more when we work together, and we will live more happily when we love our neighbor as ourselves.

Chapter 15

HIS ANSWER
TO OUR SUFFERING

MY BELOVED SON,

Our Lord is concerned about every aspect of our lives. He hears and is moved by our smallest sighs. We cannot overestimate how much our Lord wants to have a relationship with each one of us.

Twenty years ago when I first came to America, I worked at an apparel company. In two years I was able to start my own small retail clothing business in Manhattan. Within a year, my business developed some regular customers and began steadily growing. Tragically, however, a fire destroyed the entire five-story building that housed my store, reducing it all to ash. Overnight I lost everything I had built. I anguished over my loss. The weight of my suffering—both mental and financial—was so great that even to this day it is hard for me to write about the despair I felt. This was the most difficult time of my life, but God was there to instill in me the courage and hope that sustained me.

Eventually, I was able to move my business to a better location.

God's Big Picture

For the next ten years, my business continued to prosper and grow until it was time to renew the lease. The landlord was doubling my current rent, which in effect was like telling me to "move out." I tried to explain my situation to the landlord, that I had invested lots of money into my business and had built relationships with many clients and kept a good relationship with the landlord as well, but he was hearing none of it. I seethed with anger at the landlord's greed, but I knew that I had no choice but to close my shop. At that time, I thought it would be impossible to recover financially because the damage was too great, and yet God soon led me to still better things.

I fell to my knees and prayed, "Lord, please help me through this! Take away my anxiety." Even while I prayed, an unpleasant thought crept into my consciousness. Thinking of my landlord, I wondered, "Lord, why do You allow wicked men to prosper?" There was no measure of thankfulness in my prayer for the ten successful years I had experienced. Rather, I could think only of the injustice I felt had been done to me as I selfishly complained to God.

I had no understanding of God's greater plan for me and how valuable it is to experience trial and suffering, for it is through trial and suffering that God blesses us, strengthening us so we can be used for His greater plan.

It was while reading in the book of Isaiah one day that I realized how disobedient I had been.

> Remember this, fix it in mind, take it to heart, you rebels. Remember the former things, those of long ago; I am God, and there is no other; I am God, and there is none like me. I make known the end from the beginning, from ancient times, what is still to come. I say: My purpose will stand, and I will do all that I please. From the east I summon a bird of prey; from a far-off land, a man to fulfill my purpose. What I have said, that will I bring about; what I have planned, that will I do.
>
> —Isaiah 46:8-11 NIV

The Lord spoke to my heart: "Think about the times when you first came to America. Have you forgotten all the things I've done for you? I protected you from flood and flame. I heard your cries, down to even the slightest sigh. You have been rebellious and weak willed. Stand firm and remember all the things I have done for you. What I have planned, that will I do."

Humble Yourself

I was humbled upon realizing my selfishness. "Lord, thank You," I prayed. "Please forgive me for being foolish and not understanding Your plans."

The voice in my heart continued, "You ask why the wicked prosper. Do not concern yourself with others, but be mindful that you walk the right path. Be true to your heart and do what is right. The path of righteousness leads toward the sunrise, becoming brighter each step of the way, while the path of wickedness is covered with a darkness so thick that those who fall don't even notice."

I humbled myself before God. "Lord, whatever pain and suffering You ask me to endure as part of Your greater plan, I will do so. Lead where You will and I will follow. I will trust that what You have planned, You will do. Please forgive my shortsightedness, my lack of understanding, and that I did not seek first Your kingdom and justice."

God is with Us

My son, even in the depths of our despair, the Lord is always with us. Love the Lord who gave His own life for us so that we can have eternal life. Love the Lord with all your heart, all your soul, and all your life.

> God is entitled to our love, why? Because he gave himself for us despite the fact that we are so undeserving. True love is precisely this: that it does not seek its own interests. And how much does he love us? He so loved the world that he gave his only son; he laid down his life for us.
> —Bernard of Clairvaux (1090-1153)

Yes, God loves us so much that He was willing to sacrifice His son to redeem us. God does not ignore our suffering, yet when we do suffer we expect God to immediately solve our problems, and we become resentful when He doesn't, even though it is for our own good. Our heavenly Father stands with us in our times of trial, teaching us perseverance, fortifying our character, and maintaining our hope.

He watches everything we do, hears every whisper we make, and knows the secrets we seek to hide.

> You know when I sit and when I rise; you perceive my thoughts from afar. You discern my going out and my lying down; you are familiar with all my ways.
> —Psalm 139:2-3 NIV

My son, if we sincerely commit ourselves to God and seek first His kingdom and righteousness, all of our pain and suffering will disappear as our spirit rejoices in Christ. Take comfort in what God has promised, "What I have planned, that will I do."

Chapter 16

A RIGHT RELATIONSHIP WITH GOD

MY BELOVED SON,

Until we acknowledge our sinful nature and repent for our sins, we cannot enter into a right relationship with God. Therefore, the first step in developing a right relationship with God is to be repentant. By repenting of our sins we begin to tear down the wall that separates us from God.

> Nothing in all creation is hidden from God's sight. Everything is uncovered and laid bare before the eyes of him to whom we must give account.
> —Hebrews 4:13 NIV

Relationship is Formed in Repentance

When the initial fire of my love for God began to burn out, it so happened that my church declared

"Repentance Prayer Week." The idea for a week of repentance came from the Mizpah movement that began during the Philistine invasion of Israel in the days of Samuel. In an appeal for God's aid in turning back the invasion, Samuel gathered all the people of Israel to the town of Mizpah to offer sacrifices and repent of their sins.

At the same time, I remembered reading Augustine's book *Confessions*, concerning the struggle of developing a right relationship with God. As I read it, I realized I had developed an unhealthy pride in my accomplishments and that I was still so consumed with chasing after my own desires that I was forgetting to repent of my many sins.

What is repentance? According to Max Lucado in his book *Grace for the Moment*, "Repentance is the decision to turn from selfish desires and seek God. It is a genuine, sincere regret that creates sorrow and moves us to admit wrong and desire to do better. It's an inward conviction that expresses itself in outward actions."[20]

I repented for all the time I had spent building a great wall between myself and God, which, I repeat, I had done without ever realizing. My heart was filled with worldly concerns and possessions that I made into idols.

> Am I now trying to win the approval of men, or of God? Or am I trying to please men? If I were still trying to please men, I would not be a servant of Christ.
>
> —Galatians 1:10 NIV

A Prayer of Repentance

I asked God to transform me and help me build a right relationship with Him.

"Lord, I have sinned against You," I prayed. "Have mercy on me and forgive me. Hear my prayer. I am weak—too weak to resist temptation. Even today I stumbled many times. I cannot hide my sins from You. I am disgusted with myself! Please, Lord, strengthen me. Grant me the wisdom, the will, and the courage to be Your faithful servant. May Your mercy and love shine upon me. You have opened my eyes to my selfishness. Now I truly understand Your love for me. I will trust You and You alone."

In my heart I could hear God say to me, "Are you trying to please me or others? Are you seeking joy from me or from others?"

"Lord, from this day on I will not seek approval and recognition from others; my joy will come only from You. In ignorance and pride I have turned from You! My heart has not wept. My pillow has not been soaked with tears. I have not called out Your name to the point that I feel the pain of longing through my bones. But I vow from this moment on that I will seek joy and comfort only from You, Lord.

"I know that our tongues have the power to save life and destroy life. Lord, please forgive me for not truly loving my neighbor. I have not spoken enough good words to save life. Instead, I have been a hypocrite, wearing a mask with a smiling face, praising and flattering my neighbor while underneath my true face was twisted with criticism and judgment.

"Lord, You have called on us to be Your witness to the ends of the earth. I confess that I have not served You well. While publicly I spoke of my love for You, my actions failed to live up to my rhetoric. I lacked the courage to truly give my life to You.

"Have mercy on me, Lord. Forgive my lack of faith. Too often did I doubt Your authority. Make me an empty vessel and fill me with Your love. Through my repentance I want to be free in Christ—free from my sin, free to live a life of service to You. For You alone are worthy . . . and the universe cannot contain Your grandeur."

God's Grandeur

THE WORLD is charged with the grandeur of God.
It will flame out, like shining from shook foil;
It gathers to a greatness, like the ooze of oil
Crushed. Why do men then now not reck his rod?
Generations have trod, have trod, have trod;
And all is seared with trade; bleared,
smeared with toil;
And wears man's smudge and shares man's smell:
the soil
Is bare now, nor can foot feel, being shod.

And for all this, nature is never spent;
There lies the dearest freshness deep down things;
And though the last lights off the black West went

Oh, morning, at the brown brink eastward, springs—
Because the Holy Ghost over the bent
World broods with warm breast and with ah!
bright wings.[21]

—Gerard Manley Hopkins
(1844-1889)

My son, I hope that my prayer of repentance has touched your heart. If you ever stray from God, as I have, I pray that you remember my prayer and that it will lead you to acknowledge God's grandeur and confess your sins once again. For it is through repentance that we renew our spirit and develop a right relationship with God.

Chapter 17

EVEN IF HE DOESN'T

MY BELOVED SON,

> Be joyful always; pray continually; give thanks in all circumstances, for this is God's will for you in Christ Jesus.
> —1 Thessalonians 5:16-18 NIV

What the apostle Paul admonishes us to do is easier said than done. At times we may feel like we are wandering aimlessly through a desert, and yet we have been instructed to be joyful, pray continually, and give thanks in all circumstances.

Materialism Stands in the Way

How can we be "joyful, pray continually, and give thanks" when the media floods us with materialistic

messages, continually offering to sell us the thing
that will make us happy? In the midst of this sensory
bombardment, it's easy to forget that we were created
for a divine purpose.

In his book *25 Hours*, Constantine Virgil Gheorghiu
(1916-1992), a Romanian writer, writes that modern
man has lost the value of being human. We have been
poisoned by materialism. Even if the Messiah returns,
he writes, many people won't be saved because they are
living in the hour after the final hour—the twenty-fifth
hour.

A similar sentiment is found in "The Waste Land," the
famous poem penned by T. S. Eliot (1888-1965). In one
of the poem's sections, "April Is The Cruelest Month,"
Eliot depicts the purposelessness of modern life.

The Waste Land

April Is the Cruelest Month

April is the cruelest month, breeding
Lilacs out of the dead land, mixing
Memory and desire, stirring
Dull roots with spring rain.
Winter kept us warm, covering
Earth in forgetful snow, feeding
A little life with dried tubers.[22]

—T. S. Eliot

While Eliot was likely drawing on images of the
devastated wasteland that was Western Europe after four

years of trench warfare in World War I (1914-1918), his actual target was the moral and spiritual sterility of western civilization. Although the tone of "The Waste Land" is one of despair, I think Eliot hints that the recognition of our moral and spiritual ruin could be the starting point for revitalization and resurrection.

But if we desire true revitalization and resurrection, we must turn to God. For us to boldly overcome a world filled with temptations, we must strive to "be joyful always; pray continually; and give thanks in all circumstances." They say a true believer is one who wins all of his spiritual battles. It is disheartening, then, to note how often we are defeated on the spiritual battlefield. We are not alone.

Heed Poor Examples

The Bible contains many examples of men who lost their greatest spiritual battles.

Samson

At birth, Samson was set apart as a Nazirite—a member of an ascetic sect within Judaism. For years, Samson was faithful to the Naziritic code and served Israel as a judge. But he fell under the sway of Delilah, who was a Philistine. The Philistines were traditional enemies of the Israelites. Delilah tricked Samson into revealing that the secret of his strength was his hair. Samson was soon captured and delivered into the hands of the Philistines as a slave.

Achan

During the first battle for the ancient city of Ai, the Israelites were defeated because a soldier named Achan surreptitiously stole some valuables from the city that he intended to keep for himself, in violation of God's command to bring such items to the temple. So even though the Israelites vastly outnumbered the lesser force from Ai, they were nonetheless routed in battle.

> When you ask, you do not receive, because you ask with wrong motives, that you may spend what you get on your pleasures.
> —James 4:3 NIV

Jonah

Most everyone is familiar with the story of Jonah, who, the Bible tells us, was swallowed by a big fish. But that is just part of the story. Jonah's attempt to flee from God's command to prophesy to the city of Nineveh led him into that predicament.

Thomas

The New Testament gives the example of Thomas, the disciple who refused to believe that Jesus had been resurrected until he could put his hands into Jesus' wounds.

> [The resurrected Jesus said to him], "Because you have seen me, you have believed; blessed are those who have not seen and yet have believed.
> —John 20:29 NIV

Demas

Lastly for this short list, we have Demas, an associate of Paul's who accompanied him on his mission trips. The temptations of the world proved too great for Demas, and he forsook the life of a missionary with Paul for the physical comforts of this world.

Resist Temptation

If we examine ourselves honestly, we will see our own spiritual failures reflected in the biblical figures cited above, for it is not easy to follow Jesus. Sin is always standing in the way, separating us from God. And sin is easy, requiring nothing more than acting first and foremost for ourselves. But following Jesus requires discipline, perseverance, selflessness, and a faith that often flies in the face of the reason of the world. But only when we resist the temptation to sin do we draw closer to Jesus.

Rejoice in the Lord

When the Israelites were under the rule of Babylon, the prophet Habakkuk was still able to offer praise to God.

> Though the fig tree does not bud and there are no grapes on the vines, though the olive crop fails and the fields produce no food, though there are no sheep in the pen and no cattle in the stalls, yet I will rejoice in the LORD, I will be joyful in God my Savior.
> —Habakkuk 3:17-18 NIV

Even if God doesn't answer our prayers when we would like, we must remember that sometimes the meaning behind His plan will remain a mystery to us. For God is not bound by space, time, and human reasoning. God said as much when He spoke through Isaiah, proclaiming,

> "For my thoughts are not your thoughts, neither are your ways my ways," declares the LORD. "As the heavens are higher than the earth, so are my ways higher than your ways and my thoughts than your thoughts."
> —Isaiah 55:8-9 NIV

Surrender to God

Having the faith to say "Even if He doesn't" means surrendering yourself and living by the will of God.

> He himself bore our sins in his body on the tree, so that we might die to sins and live for righteousness.
> —1 Peter 2:24 NIV

Follow Good Examples

The Bible is full of heroes and martyrs who surrendered themselves so that they might live by the will of God.

Queen Esther

Queen Esther was willing to risk her own life for the sake of the people of Israel. She left her fate up to God, declaring, "If I perish, I perish." Her courage helped save the Israelites from mass slaughter.

Shadrach, Meshach, and Abednego

When Shadrach, Meshach, and Abednego were about to be thrown into the fiery furnace by King Nebuchadnezzar of Babylon, they confronted him.

> If we are thrown into the blazing furnace, the God we serve is able to save us from it, and he will rescue us from your hand, O king. But even if he does not, we want you to know, O king, that we will not serve your gods or worship the image of gold you have set up.
> —Daniel 3:17-18 NIV

Because of their faith, God saved them from the blazing furnace without so much as a singed hair.

Abraham

Abraham's willingness to obey God's command to sacrifice his only son Isaac made him the father of all believers. Despite incomprehensible suffering—losing his family, his livestock, and his health—Job never cursed God, and his endurance ultimately earned him even greater blessings from God.

Stephen

Stephen's fearless confession for Christ before the Sanhedrin enabled him to see the glory of God as heaven opened up before him. When Paul and Silas were thrown into prison in Philippi, they prayed and sang hymns to God. Because of their complete trust in God, the earth shook, the prison doors flew open, and their chains came undone.

As all of the above examples show, when we give our hearts wholly to God, not only will we be a joy to Him, but He will be by our side.

Our life on earth is a journey, and our time is precious and fleeting. However, in the long hours of the day we often lose sight of that fact and live each day seeking for the comfort of the body. All men are like grass, and their glory is like the flowers. The grass withers and the flowers fade (from Isaiah 40:6-7). As we get older, we often lose the ideals and hopes that sustained us in our youth. But when we live in Jesus Christ, even though our body ages, our spirit is constantly being renewed.

Youth

Youth is not a time of life; it is a state of mind; it is not a matter of rosy cheeks, red lips and supple knees; it is a matter of the will, a quality of the imagination, a vigor of the emotions; it is the freshness of the deep springs of life.

Youth means a temperamental predominance of courage over timidity of the appetite, for adventure over the love of ease. This often exists in a man of sixty more than a body of twenty. Nobody grows old merely by a number of years. We grow old by deserting our ideals.

Years may wrinkle the skin, but to give up enthusiasm wrinkles the soul. Worry, fear, self-distrust bows the heart and turns the spirit back to dust. Whether sixty or sixteen, there is in every human being's heart the lure of wonder, the unfailing child-like appetite of what's next, and the joy of the game of living. In the center of your heart and my heart there is a wireless station; so long as it receives messages of beauty, hope, cheer, courage and power from men and from the Infinite, so long are you young.

When the aerials are down, and your spirit is covered with snows of cynicism and the ice of pessimism, then you are grown old, even at twenty, but as long as your aerials are up, to catch the waves of optimism, there is hope you may die young at eighty.[23]

—Samuel Ullman (1840-1924)

Rev. C. H. Spurgeon (1834-1892) stated that there are two types of believers: Those whose faith is small and those whose faith is large. Those with a small faith only look to heaven, while those with a large faith bring heaven down to this world.

My son, whether or not God answers your prayer as you would like, you must be obedient to God and wait for the Lord's time. In the meantime, try to have a bigger faith and work to bring heaven to this world.

Chapter 18

INDEBTED TO JESUS

MY BELOVED SON,

Through the grace of our Lord, who sacrificed His Son Jesus on the cross, we have been saved from our sins. When I think of the image of Jesus hanging on the cross at Calvary, I am reminded of the cross that hangs above the altar at my church. That cross is hidden behind a black curtain during the season of Lent, creating an air of solemnity over our Easter Sunday worship.

To think how Jesus suffered so greatly for us overwhelms my heart. What did we do to deserve such sacrifice? How could we be so loved by a God who is infinitely beyond our understanding?

> I am the good shepherd; I know my sheep and my sheep know me—just as the Father knows me and

I know the Father—and I lay down my life for the
sheep.

—John 10:14-15, NIV

Jesus Is Our Good Shepherd

Like a good shepherd, Jesus guides and protects his
flock—you, me, and everyone—prone to wander as we
are, to seek our own way in this world. Jesus is always
there to lead us back to the love of the Father.

In one of his letters, Paul describes the condition of
men who choose to deny and disobey God even though
the truth about God has been made plain to them.

> Furthermore, since they did not think it worthwhile
> to retain the knowledge of God, he gave them over
> to a depraved mind, to do what ought not to be
> done. They have become filled with every kind of
> wickedness, evil, greed and depravity. They are full of
> envy, murder, strife, deceit and malice. They are gos-
> sips, slanderers, God-haters, insolent, arrogant and
> boastful; they invent ways of doing evil; they disobey
> their parents; they are senseless, faithless, heartless,
> ruthless. Although they know God's righteous decree
> that those who do such things deserve death, they
> not only continue to do these very things but also
> approve of those who practice them.
>
> —Romans 1:28-32 NIV

The truth is that even though we are created in
God's image, we often fail to live up to our potential,
and through sin we bring destruction upon ourselves.
Therefore, we need to be healed through the blood of

Jesus Christ so that our relationship with the Father can be made right.

Through Christ's death and resurrection we are born anew in spirit, into light and into eternal life.

> You were taught, with regard to your former way of life, to put off your old self, which is being corrupted by its deceitful desires; to be made new in the attitude of your minds; and to put on the new self, created to be like God in true righteousness and holiness.
> —Ephesians 4:22-24 NIV

The Holy Spirit is Our Helper

However much we try, putting off our old self cannot be done by our willpower alone. Only with the help of the Holy Spirit can we suppress ourselves so that Christ may live in us. This is a process. It's not a one-time event, but one that needs to be worked on constantly through prayer, self-restraint, and good works.

I have seen faith described as this acronym:

Forsaking
All
I
Trust
Him

God is Our Faithful Father

Faith is forsaking everything I have and trusting God completely. When the focus of our life changes from self-centered to God-centered, we will be blessed through grace with a peace that cannot be found anywhere else.

As Christians, we can bear the fruit of love, for we have been instructed to love one another as we love ourselves. In fact, God is love.

> Dear friends, let us love one another, for love comes from God. Everyone who loves has been born of God and knows God. Whoever does not love does not know God, because God is love.
>
> —1 John 4:7-8 NIV

Paradoxical Commandments

People are often unreasonable, illogical,
And self-centered;
Forgive them anyway.
If you are kind,
People may accuse you of selfish, ulterior motives;
Be kind anyway . . .
If you are honest and frank,
people may cheat you;
Be honest and frank anyway.
What you spend years building,
someone could destroy overnight;
Build anyway.
If you find serenity and happiness,
They may be jealous;
Be happy anyway.
The good you do today,
People will often forget tomorrow;
Do good anyway.

Give the world the best you have,
and it may never be enough;
Give the world the best you've got anyway.[24]
—Author Unknown

Nearly two thousand years have passed since Christ was crucified, yet we remain forever in His debt for the forgiveness we have received. As God has forgiven us, so too should we forgive our neighbors. Let us therefore shine God's light of love and forgiveness into the dark corners of the world.

Section Four
Praise the Lord

Chapter 19

LIVING WITH THE END IN MIND

MY BELOVED SON,

Our life on earth is short, so live each day to the fullest. Don't dwell on past failures. Instead focus on the present and be hopeful for the future. Doing so will help you to invest each day with purpose and meaning.

Three Questions

The great Russian writer Tolstoy is best known for his epic novel *War and Peace*. Less well known is a short story he wrote titled "Three Questions" (1903). The questions at the heart of "Three Questions" concern a king's search for the meaning of life:

> *When is the right time to do things?*
> Now—it is the only time we can control.

Who is the most important person?
The person standing before us, because we never know
if we will encounter anyone else.
What is the most important thing to do?
To do right by the person we are with at any given
moment, for that purpose alone were we created.

Time

I'm sure you've heard the saying "There is no time like the present." What this saying tells us is that we should not put aside for tomorrow what can be done today. As I mentioned earlier, when we are young, we are less aware that our time is limited. We think of death as remote—something that happens to older people—and we put it in the back of our minds and quickly return to the comfort and familiarity of our routine. Was this earlier too?

However, the truth is that none of us knows when and how we will face our final day of life. That's why life should be about making the best of the time God has given us. Waking up each morning to receive a new day is one of the most heartwarming and exhilarating experiences in life. If you treat each day as if it could be your last, seeking to bring God's kingdom to earth, loving your neighbor, and bringing glory to God, you will truly live life to the fullest.

Chronos and Kairos

Ancient philosophers distinguished between two types of time. One is the time by which we measure the hours, days, and years of our lives, which is called *chronos*. The second is God's eternal time, which is known as *kairos*. Here on earth, we live within the narrow window of time (chronos) that God has granted to us. But we will spend eternity (kairos) with God in heaven.

God has given us the gift of free will that we might do with our time what we will. We are free to serve Him or serve ourselves. As we read in Ecclesiastes, however, it is very clear who is our ultimate sovereign.

> There is a time for everything, and a season for every activity under heaven:
> a time to be born and a time to die,
> a time to plant and a time to uproot,
> a time to kill and a time to heal,
> a time to tear down and a time to build,
> a time to weep and a time to laugh,
> a time to mourn and a time to dance,
> a time to scatter stones and a time to gather them,
> a time to embrace and a time to refrain,
> a time to search and a time to give up,
> a time to keep and a time to throw away,
> a time to tear and a time to mend,
> a time to be silent and a time to speak,
> a time to love and a time to hate,
> a time for war and a time for peace.
>
> I know that there is nothing better for men than to be happy and do good while they live. That everyone may eat and drink, and find satisfaction in all his toil—this is the gift of God. I know that everything God does will endure forever; nothing can be added

to it and nothing taken from it. God does it so that
men will revere him.

—Ecclesiastes 3:1-8, 12-14 NIV

According to John Calvin (1509-1564), if we do
not have the hope of eternity after death, we are no
better than a beast. That's because life without the
consideration of death is a perpetual state of ignorance.
By contrast, when we live our life with the end in mind,
we will not take one day for granted. Rather, we can
pause and reflect on whether we are leading a righteous
life.

Always remember that life is a precious gift that
God has entrusted to us for a short time. It is up to us
to make the most of the time we have, bringing glory
and honor to God by loving one another.

Chapter 20

PLEASING GOD

MY BELOVED SON,

As Christians, we are often of two minds: we sincerely desire to serve God, but more often than not, we selfishly serve our own interests. These two irreconcilable desires are constantly competing within us, creating much confusion.

Resist Selfishness

The more often we submit to selfishness, the more difficult it becomes to resist. We are rational creatures, and we can rationalize any selfish action. But worldly success is fleeting and unfulfilling. If we want to live our lives for our Lord, we must think about what pleases God.

The LORD your God is with you, he is mighty to save.
He will take great delight in you, he will quiet you
with his love, he will rejoice over you with singing.

—Zephaniah 3:17 NIV

Know Your Purpose

What is our purpose in life? How we answer that
question (and whether we can answer the question)
both reflects and determines the type of life we lead. As
Christians, we answer that we were created to be like
God's only Son, Jesus, and our purpose is to carry out
God's will. We should not seek to live comfortably or to
measure our accomplishments and possessions against
those of others. Rather, a truly blessed life is one in
which we serve God and seek to enact His will in our
lives, living humbly and faithfully.

Think about this: the same God who carved
mountains that are miles high and filled oceans that are
miles deep, the same God who laid the foundation for
the earth and set the stars in the sky can count the hairs
on your head!

God knows you intimately and loves you more than
you can possibly imagine. There is no issue too great that
you can't lay before Him. Turn to Him for strength and
support in times of hardship. While it may be difficult
to appreciate or understand at the time, God is always at
work in our lives, especially when we are going through
difficult times.

Throughout the Bible, God is referred to as a father.
Like a loving father, He delights in us when we are
obedient and grieves when we are not.

And do not grieve the Holy Spirit of God, with whom you were sealed for the day of redemption.
—Ephesians 4:30 NIV

Know God

What joy it brings to know that God is always with us! For true wisdom and joy come from knowing God.

You have made known to me the path of life; you will fill me with joy in your presence, with eternal pleasures at your right hand.
—Psalm 16:11 NIV

Like a good father, God wants his children to live a life filled with joy. In fact, a joyful heart is one of the blessings we receive from the Holy Spirit when we are obedient to God. Because our purpose is to live for God, we must seek to use whatever talents and abilities we have to glorify Him. We will not always succeed. But even when we fail, God always delights when we rise up again. When we are broken in spirit, He is there to heal us. And as long as God takes pleasure from us, we receive His kingdom as a gift.

"Come, you who are blessed by my Father; take your inheritance, the kingdom prepared for you since the creation of the world."
—Matthew 25:34 NIV

Serve God

To maintain a healthy spiritual life we must resist the temptations of the secular world so as not to become hypocrites. Earlier I mentioned our ability to rationalize selfish behavior. The companion of rationalization is deception—deception of self and neighbor. But God demands sincerity from us, for only sincere words, actions, and songs of praise are pleasing to God. We may be able to fool ourselves and others with our hypocrisy, be we cannot fool God.

So I encourage you to live a life that is pleasing to God, a life of faith and love, of sacrifice and commitment to obeying God's Word, for which you will receive the joy of the Spirit.

Chapter 21

HERE I AM

MY BELOVED SON,

Always and everywhere, our Lord is with us. There was a time when I was foolish and ignored the voice of God within me asking, "Where are you?" Like the prodigal son in the gospel of Luke, I was living life my way without God. Yet even though I ignored His voice, still God was with me. Even when I immersed myself in the wisdom of philosophers like Plato, Kant, Hegel, and Nietzsche and cultivated an air of superiority, still the Lord silently waited for me, being ever patient with my rebellious behavior.

Even though I had ears that couldn't hear and eyes that couldn't see—immature as I was, God always forgave me and covered me with His love. What God earnestly desired was for me to open my eyes to faith, repent for my past, and follow His plan for my life.

When God asks, "Where are you?" He wants us to
say, "Lord, here I am." No matter the stage of life we're
in, our Lord wants us to live a fulfilling life in Christ.

I was deeply moved when Holt Choir, a children's
choir from South Korea, came to sing at my church.
Holt Choir is composed of orphans and handicapped
children. Through their songs of praise, I witnessed
God's hand at work. I saw how He lifts up the weak and
forgotten people of the world. I understood how God
takes the stone that the builders rejected and makes it
the cornerstone.

One song I found particularly moving was called
simply "I", and was written by the poet Myunghee Song,
who suffers from cerebral palsy.

I

I do not have wealth,
I do not have knowledge like others,
I do not have health like others,
But I have something that no one has,
I received the love that no one has received,
I understood what no one has understood . . .
Faithful God, I do not have what others have,
Faithful God, I have what others do not have.[25]
—Myunghee Song

Before God, our health, our knowledge, and our
possessions matter little. If we stray from God because
we do not have these things, we are foolish. God gave
each one of us different talents and abilities to do good

in this world—to help our neighbor and bring glory to Him. I want to be able to give my life to my Lord so that when I finally stand before God, I can be called a good and faithful servant.

The gospel of Luke uses the metaphor of a servant to show us the proper attitude with which we should serve God.

> "Suppose one of you had a servant plowing or looking after the sheep. Would he say to the servant when he comes in from the field, 'Come along now and sit down to eat'? Would he not rather say, 'Prepare my supper, get yourself ready and wait on me while I eat and drink; after that you may eat and drink'? Would he thank the servant because he did what he was told to do? So you also, when you have done everything you were told to do, should say, 'We are unworthy servants; we have only done our duty.'"
>
> —Luke 17:7-10 NIV

Although we are unworthy servants before our Lord, He has called each one of us and wants to do His work through us. And now I repent that I have not been a good servant, and I humbly kneel down before my Lord and pray that He will help me spread Christ's love.

Prayer of St. Francis of Assisi

Lord, make me an instrument of your peace.
Where there is hatred, let me sow love;
where there is injury, pardon;
where there is doubt, faith;

where there is despair, hope;
where there is darkness, light;
and where there is sadness, joy.

O, Divine Master,
grant that I may not so much seek
to be consoled as to console;
to be understood as to understand;
to be loved as to love.

For it is in giving that we receive;
it is in pardoning that we are pardoned;
and it is in dying that we are born to eternal life.[26]

—St. Francis of Assisi (1181-1226)

A true Christian carries the Spirit of Christ within him at all times. I want to rid myself of my past failings wherein I projected the image of a godly man even though I did not live like one. I want to devote my life to God, the life to which I—and you—as Christians have been called.

But you, man of God, flee from all of this, and pursue righteousness, godliness, faith, love, endurance and gentleness. Fight the good fight of the faith. Take hold of the eternal life to which you were called when you made your good confession in the presence of many witnesses.

—1 Timothy 6:11-12 NIV

I am grateful for the grace that enables this unworthy servant to be called a "man of God." I will live my life as Christ's witness and fight the good fight of faith, always doing my best to spread the good news of love and salvation.

Chapter 22

FADING
CHRISTMAS CAROL

MY BELOVED SON,

It saddens me that Christmas carols are fading away in America, a land that was first settled by the Pilgrims—men and women who fled England, seeking the freedom to worship. These days in department stores you'll hear endless replays of "Frosty the Snowman" and "Rudolph the Red Nosed Reindeer," but you'll rarely, if ever, hear "Silent Night" or "Away in a Manger."

Recent years have seen the emergence of an anti-Christian movement that seeks to eliminate all traces of Christianity from public life. The words "Merry Christmas" have been replaced with "Happy Holidays" or "Season's Greetings." Towns and cities across the country have passed ordinances forbidding the display of the Nativity on public property. Instead of a celebration of the birth of Jesus Christ, Christmas has become like any other secular holiday, only with more rampant commercialism attached.

Life, liberty, and the pursuit of happiness are the basic human rights proclaimed in the Declaration of Independence and guaranteed in the United States Constitution. These "unalienable" human rights are granted to man by God. In other words, the fundamental rights that we enjoy as Americans have their basis in the God of the Bible.

This intertwining of faith and politics was due in part to men like John Witherspoon (1723-1794), an ordained minister and president of Princeton, who strongly believed that Christian faith was essential to liberty. Witherspoon risked his life, as did many others, when he put his name to the Declaration of Independence in 1787. Even though he was a Protestant minister, he taught philosophy based on enlightenment, literature, history, and science and allowed freedom of ideology. He also later served as a delegate to New Jersey's ratification of the Constitution. American democracy was therefore informed by Christian faith for the purpose of protecting the individual's rights.

Prior to the Bolshevik Revolution of 1917, Christianity had flourished in Russia. Under atheist, Communist rule, however, Christianity was aggressively attacked and Christians were persecuted. After the death of its first Communist leader, Vladimir Lenin (1870-1924), Joseph Stalin (1879-1953) consolidated power and ruled as a merciless dictator. Under his rule, millions of Russians lost their lives to persecution, famine, and war. Russia lost its collective soul when it attempted to replace Jesus Christ with Lenin and Stalin, who viewed man as only the sum of his material wants. The atheist, materialist utopia they tried to bring about has largely been consigned to the dustbin of history.

When we attempt to live without God, He will eventually destroy everything we have achieved, whether as individuals or as a society. History is littered with the ashes of civilizations that seemed invincible in their day: the Egyptians, Babylonians, and Romans, to name but a few. Even a nation as wealthy and powerful as America can fall if we abandon God. This is why I'm so saddened to watch as Christmas becomes just another secular holiday; another reason for retailers to offer special sales.

Charles Dickens' (1812-1870) classic novella *A Christmas Carol* features the miserly, cynical Ebenezer Scrooge, who has no use for Christmas, charity, family, or anything that can't be tabulated on a ledger sheet. After being visited on Christmas Eve by the ghost of his former partner and three other spirits, Scrooge wakes up on Christmas morning a changed man. Like snow falling from the December sky, God's blessings rained down from heaven and opened his heart.

As the true meaning of Christmas recedes from public consciousness and is replaced with crass commercialism, we are becoming more like the people Jesus described in the book of Matthew.

"To what can I compare this generation? They are like children sitting in the marketplaces and calling out to others: 'We played the flute for you, and you

did not dance; we sang a dirge, and you did not
mourn.'"

—Matthew 11:16-17 NIV

In the poem "Epitaph to a Dog," the English Romantic
poet George Gordon, Lord Byron (1788-1824), uses wit
to show how the finest qualities of human nature are
best exemplified in a dog.

Epitaph to a Dog

Near this spot
are deposited the remains of one
who possessed beauty without vanity
strength without insolence
courage without ferocity
and all the virtues of man without his vices.
This praise, which would be unmeaning flattery
if inscribed over human ashes,
is but a just tribute to the memory of
Boatswain, a dog
who was born at Newfoundland, May, 1803,
and died at Newstead Abbey, Nov. 18, 1808.[27]

—George Gordon, Lord Byron (1788-1824)

The fading of Christmas carols from the public
sphere saddens what should be a joyous celebration
of the birth of Jesus, who came from heaven to save
us all. I sincerely hope that I will live to see the day

when Christmas carols can once again ring out from everywhere as they used to, bringing joy to our hearts and proclaiming peace on earth and goodwill toward men.

Chapter 23

SCIENCE, RELIGION, AND HUMAN KNOWLEDGE

MY BELOVED SON,

As our civilization continues to make breakthroughs in science and technology, we should not forget to thank God for giving us the knowledge and wisdom to achieve all that we have. However, it is heartbreaking to see instead how pride in our scientific and technological accomplishments has caused us to turn further away from God when humility is really what is called for. For no matter how technologically advanced our civilization may be, from the vantage point of God, the Creator of the universe, our accomplishments are insignificant.

The Mind of God

We need to be reminded of the infinite chasm that separates our human knowledge from the mind of God.

"Who is this that darkens my counsel with words
without knowledge? Brace yourself like a man; I will
question you, and you shall answer me. Where were
you when I laid the earth's foundation? Tell me, if
you understand. Who marked off its dimensions?
Surely you know! Who stretched a measuring line
across it? On what were its footings set, or who laid its
cornerstone—while the morning stars sang together
and all the angels shouted for joy?"

—Job 38:2-7 NIV

Yes, through science we learn the secrets of the
universe one by one, but God warns us through Job to
be mindful of our overweening pride, because for all we
understand through science, we know only that which
God has chosen to reveal. The mind of God is infinitely
beyond our ability to grasp.

The Minds of Scientists

The Greek philosopher Aristotle (384-322 B.C.) believed that if two objects of different weights were dropped
simultaneously, the heavier object would fall faster than
the lighter one. However, two thousand years later, Italian
physicist Galileo Galilei (1564-1642) disproved Aristotle's
theory. Galileo conducted an experiment in which he
dropped two balls of different weights from the Tower of
Pisa. What he discovered was that regardless of weight,
the balls fell at the same rate of speed.

In Europe in the early sixteenth century, the prevail-
ing theory of how the solar system was organized claimed
that the earth was the center of the universe. However, in

his book *On the Revolutions of the Celestial Spheres,* which was published the year of his death, the great astronomer Copernicus (1473-1543) posited his heliocentric theory that the sun is in fact the center of the universe. Although initially rejected by the Catholic Church, Copernicus' theory eventually became accepted.

After this, Galilei and Kepler proved the theory.

Later, Isaac Newton (1642-1727) became a forefather in present science through his universal law of gravitation, the laws of motion. Newton realized that the gravity that pulled down the apple is greater, as is the power that rotates the moon. Then Robert Boyle (1627-91) introduced the word "atom" in his theory. Many other discoveries followed: steam by James Watt (1736-1819), dynamite by Alfred Nobel (1833-96), telephone by Graham Bell (1847-1922), and the automobile by Gottilieb Daimler (1834-1900) and Karl Benz (1844-1929). Antoine Hanri Becaquerel (1852-1908) discovered radiation from uranium. Marie Curie (1867-1934) discovered radium, which is the substance for radiation. The twentieth century's greatest inventor Thomas Edison (1847-1931) invented more than thirteen thousand items, such as the light bulb, gramophone, motion pictures, and electricity. The brothers, Wilbur Wright (1867-1912) and Orville Wright (1871-1948), were the first successful ones to fly, Guglielmo Marconi (1874-1937) succeeded in wireless, John Baird (1888-1946) in television, and Wallace Carothers (1896-1937) in discovering nylon. The twenty century's best physics scholar Albert Einstein (1879-1955) completed his universal relativity theory in 1916. He changed the world's views on cosmos, space, substance, and energy and opened a new era in physics. Wernher Von Braun (1912-1977) made the first rocket.

Within hundreds of years, science and technology advanced rapidly, and we now live in an era of heightened technology. For example, we live in an automatic action world with automatic sliding doors, automatic water taps, and automatic lights in doorsteps. This automatic technology is based on traveling infrared light. The amount is very small, but human beings release infrared light as well.

We should not forget that science exists only within the power of Almighty God. When science is confronted with its limitations, we should understand that perhaps God is permitting us to know only as much as He wants us to know.

We in the developed world have been blessed with technological advances that make life less burdensome and more comfortable and enjoyable. Automobiles, air conditioning, and personal computers are just some of the advances that have made our lives easier. However, this convenience and comfort can come at a cost. If we're not careful, this increased comfort can make us spiritually lazy as we become less dependent on God.

Technology carries with it the temptation to distract. After all, it's much easier to turn on the television or surf the Internet than it is to concentrate on God's Word or to earnestly pray. So, while science and technology have made our lives better and easier, we must be careful that they do not become a replacement for our Lord and

Father. That's why it's so important to renew our spirit in His Word each day of our lives.

> For if you live according to the sinful nature, you will die; but if by the Spirit you put to death the misdeeds of the body, you will live.
> —Romans 8:13 NIV

Just as the pull of gravity exerts its force on all objects, so too does God's dominion include all of creation. That is, as beings created by God, we exist within God's purview. If we live solely according to our individual will, our spirit will be shut off from God. However, if we live by God's wisdom and according to His will, our spirit will experience new life and peace. As great as our advances in science and technology may be to us, they are like grains of sand on the seashore to the God who created us.

Chapter 24

PRAISE THE LORD

MY BELOVED SON,

As we sing in t*he Doxology* by Thomas Ken (1637-1711)

> Praise God, from whom all blessings flow;
> Praise Him, all creatures here below;
> Praise Him above, ye heavenly host;
> Praise Father, Son, and Holy Ghost. Amen.

Praising God glorifies our Creator, from whom all blessings flow, and renews and strengthens our spirit.

> Why are you downcast, O my soul? Why so disturbed within me? Put your hope in God, for I will yet praise him, my Savior and my God.
>
> —Psalm 42:5 NIV

Prayers of Praise

When you and I lift praise to God, He blesses us by filling our hearts with joy. If we praise God when we are full of sorrow, He comforts us with His gentle hand. If we praise God when we feel frustrated, He encourages us to overcome. If we praise God when we are in despair, He fills us with hope. Whenever we offer praise to God, He is there to receive our prayer and His blessings flow like a river of grace.

Praise the LORD.
Praise God in his sanctuary;
praise him in his mighty heavens.
Praise him for his acts of power;
praise him for his surpassing greatness.
Praise him with the sounding of the trumpet,
praise him with the harp and lyre,
praise him with tambourine and dancing,
praise him with the strings and flute,
praise him with the clash of cymbals,
praise him with resounding cymbals.
Let everything that has breath praise the LORD.
Praise the LORD.

—Psalm 150:1-6 NIV

Almighty Lord, I praise You.
All greatness, power, and glory are Yours.
Everything belongs to You.
All authority and power lie in Your mighty hands.
My life belongs to You.
With a heart full of gratitude, I offer You this prayer of thanks for all that I have experienced in this life

You have given me—the joy as well as the sorrow, the triumphs and the failures.

My soul desires only to praise You, Lord—

whether with joy or in sorrow, uplifted with hope or bowed in despair.

Whatever path lies before me, whatever adversity I may face,

I will never cease to praise You, for I know You are with me.

Almighty Lord!

Sovereign God, You are holy.

Your power is endless.

Your plans are perfect.

Let me praise You, Lord,

with all my heart and soul,

with true wholeheartedness.

Lord, renew my spirit!

Let my life be a joy to You.

How can I describe all of Your great love with my limited words?

How can I even praise You with these tainted lips?

Praise the Lord, my soul, praise the Lord!

With all my heart, for as long as I breathe,

I will praise the Lord!

ENDNOTES

Chapter Two - Cultivate Good Habits

1. Stephen R. Covey, *The Seven Habits of Highly Effective People* (New York: New York Free Press, 2004), 48-52.

Chapter Three - Always Be Prepared

2. General Douglas MacArthur, "A Father's Prayer."
3. Edgar A. Guest, "See it Through."

Chapter Four - Paint a Big Picture

4. Gordon MacDonald, *A Resilient Life*, (Nashville: Thomas Nelson, Inc., 2004), 147-148, 168-170.
5. Langston Hughes, "Mother to Son."

6. Henri J. M. Nouwen, *Here and Now* (New York: The Crossroad Publishing Company, 2003), 130-131.

Chapter Five - Lead a Victorious Life

7. C. S. Lewis, *The Problem of Pain*, (New York: Harper Collins Publishers, 1996), 88-89.

Chapter Seven - Always Give Thanks

8. Brother Lawrence, *The Practice of the Presence of God* (Brewster, Masschursetts:: Paraclete Press, 1985), 66-67, 145-146.

9. Dietrich Bonhoeffer, *Letters and Papers from Prison,* (London: SCM Press 1967), 99.

Chapter Eight - Beautiful Person

10. Madeline Bridges. "Life's Mirror."

11. Robert Bridges, "I Love All Beauteous Things."

Chapter Ten - For Your Lonely Neighbor

12. Blaise Pascal, *Pensees* (London: Penguin Books Ltd., 1995), 33-36.

13. Helen Steiner Rice. "Learn to Rest So Your Life Will Be Blest."

Chapter Eleven - Pray as You Get Busier

14. Richard J. Foster, *Prayer* (New York: Harper Collins Publisher, 1992), 126, 127.

Chapter Twelve - Overcome Trials

15. Thomas à Kempis, *Of the Imitation of Christ* (USA: Barnes & Noble Books, 2004), 21-23, 143-145.
16. Rick Warren, The *Purpose Driven Life* (Michigan: Zondervan, 2002), 201-207.

Chapter Thirteen - Autumn Letter

17. Ch 'un-Su Kim, "Flower."
18. Mother Teresa, *In the Heart of the World* (New York: MJF Books, 1997), 14.

Chapter Fourteen - True Neighbor

19. Young Ja Kim, "Love Your Neighbor."

Chapter Sixteen - A Right Relationship with God

20. Max Lucado, *Grace for the Moment* (Nashville: J. Countryman, 2000), 217.
21. Gerard Manley Hopkins, "God's Grandeur."

Chapter Seventeen- Even If He Doesn't

22. T. S. Elliot, "The Waste Land."

Chapter Eighteen - Indebted to Jesus

23. Samuel Ullman, "Youth."
24. Unknown. "Paradoxical Commandments."

Chapter Twenty-One - Here I Am

25. Myunghee Song, "I."
26. St. Francis of Assisi, "Prayer."

Chapter Twenty-Two-Fading Christmas Carol

27. George Gordon Lord Byron. "Epitaph to a Dog."